Forensic Firearms in Criminal Trials

Legal, Investigative, and Scientific Aspects

J. K. Sinha

CRC Press
Taylor & Francis Group
Boca Raton London New York

CRC Press is an imprint of the
Taylor & Francis Group, an **informa** business

Designed cover image: shutterstock

First edition published 2024
by CRC Press
2385 NW Executive Center Drive, Suite 320, Boca Raton FL 33431

and by CRC Press
4 Park Square, Milton Park, Abingdon, Oxon, OX14 4RN

CRC Press is an imprint of Taylor & Francis Group, LLC

ISBN: 978-1-138-49565-4 (hbk)
ISBN: 978-1-032-74546-6 (pbk)
ISBN: 978-1-351-02386-3 (ebk)

DOI: 10.4324/9781351023863

Typeset in Caslon
by codeMantra

Forensic Firearms in Criminal Trials

Over the last two-plus decades, the scientific validity of the principles that underpin identifying a firearm from recovered fired ammunition has been a core issue for the admissibility of expert evidence in criminal trials in the United States. The issues that dominated the determinative points, as they related to the scientific and technological analysis, centered around the following: the validity of uniqueness of firearms, subjective methodology, the potential rate of error, unknown statistical certainty, and unsatisfactory proficiency tests. These issues have essentially become the legal requirement for admissibility of experts' opinion on the linkage of firearms with fired ammunition, an important forensic opinion that connects the crime with the perpetrator through the weapon of offence.

In *Forensic Firearms in Criminal Trials: Legal, Investigative, and Scientific Aspects*, internationally renowned forensic firearm expert Dr J. K. Sinha provides demonstrative explanations and helpful clarifications using simple illustrative examples from scientific casework and everyday life. The goals are to:

- Prove the scientific validity of the uniqueness of identifying features of firearms
- Identify the statistical threshold to qualify and determine a corresponding match
- Debunk the misconception of subjective methodology and the potential rate of error thereof in experts' decision making and opinions
- Clarify the prevailing perception of similar, dissimilar, and insufficient marks and consequential interpretation

With certain non-technical readers in mind as well, the book provides a basic understanding of the general make-up of firearms and ammunition, the evidentiary values of commonly used firearms, fired empties, fired bullets and pellets, and scientific investigative leads that result from visual and physical evidence. Chapters cover related topics such as proficiency tests, identifying competent experts, admitted firing, and reliable and testable methodology. The book also reviews the admissibility of expert evidence in India and explains the proviso of admissibility of ballistic expert reports in criminal trials. Throughout, the author emphasizes the need for requisite forensic knowledge by the investigator aided by a competent expert for effective scientific investigation of gunfire crimes such as would aid in the proper presentation of scientific evidence at criminal trial for a successful outcome.

J. K. Sinha has a PhD in forensic science. He has been associated with this field for more than six decades in a variety of capacities. An internationally known forensic firearm expert and consultant, he has been a firearm examiner for central government for over 34 years and has served as Director-in-Charge and Head of Ballistics Division of Central Forensic Laboratory, Chandigarh, India.

Dedicated to my loving grandchildren,
Ananya, Ambika and Aryan

Contents

List of figures ix
About the author xi
Forewords xiii
Acknowledgments xv

Part I Legal aspects in criminal trials involving firearms

Chapter 1 Introduction to evidence in criminal trials involving firearms: a brief review 3
Chapter 2 Admissibility of ballistics expert evidence in criminal trials in the United States 10
Chapter 3 Admissibility of ballistics expert evidence in criminal trials in India 35

Part II Investigative aspects in criminal trials involving firearms

Chapter 4 Introduction to the investigation of gunfire crime and the basics of firearms and ammunition 43
Chapter 5 Evidentiary values of fired ammunition in criminal trials and investigative leads 50
Chapter 6 Fired projectiles as evidentiary clues in criminal trials and investigative leads 56

Chapter 7 Evidentiary values of firearms in criminal trials and investigative leads 70
Chapter 8 Eyewitness statements and investigative leads 81
Chapter 9 Investigation of admitted firing in criminal trials 89

Part III Scientific aspects in criminal trials involving firearms: identification of firearms from fired ammunition

Chapter 10 Identification of firearms from fired empties 99
Chapter 11 Identification of rifled firearms from fired bullets 108
Chapter 12 Scientific evidence vs eyewitness in criminal trials involving firearms 114

Selected references 123

Index 125

Figures

Figure 6.1a Right-handed rifling marks on fired bullets 57

Figure 6.1b Left-handed rifling marks on fired bullets 57

Figure 6.2a A perforated cap 66

Figure 6.2b A blown cap 67

Figure 6.3 Square-shaped propellants from a short-barrelled auto pistol 69

Figure 7.1 A 12-bore DBBL shotgun 72

Figure 7.2 A six-chambered revolver 73

Figure 7.3 A .315 bolt-action rifle 75

Figure 7.4 A 12-bore pump-action shotgun 77

Figure 7.5 A 7.65mm semi-automatic pistol 78

Figure 7.6 An AK47 assault rifle 79

Figure 10.1 Monogram of ICI embossed on the primer 99

Figure 10.2 Different firing pin marks but similar breech 102

Figure 10.3 Firing pin impression obtained on a lead piece by hand pressing 104

Figure 10.4a Breech marks obtained by light hammering on breech face 105

Figure 10.4b Matching of breech marks on evidence empty and test specimen 105

Figure 10.5 Deceptive breech marks created during push–fit operation of primers at the time of manufacturing 106

Figure 10.6 Double firing pin hits 107

Figure 11.1 Rifling marks on a .32 elongated lead bullet fired from under-sized (.29″) revolver 110

Figure 11.2 Straight striations on under-sized smooth-bore fired bullets 111

About the author

J. K. Sinha has a PhD in forensic science. He has been associated with this field for more than six decades in a variety of capacities. An internationally known forensic firearm consultant, he has been a firearm examiner for the federal and central government for over 34 years and has served as Director-In-Charge and Head, Ballistics Division of Central Forensic Laboratory, Chandigarh, India. He has examined more than 5,000 criminal cases involving firearms. He has visited numerous crime scenes and rendered expert guidance to enforcement and investigating agencies in the reconstruction and other forensic aspects of shooting incidents. He has testified in hundreds of courts (including military courts and judicial enquiry) as a prosecution, defence and court witness, and has assisted the court in the verification of the prosecution/defence version. His testimony on significant forensic issues has been published in law journals of court judgments and referred to as case law by practising attorneys and lawyers in India.

Dr Sinha has been actively engaged in postgraduate university teaching and research and has supervised successful PhD candidates on topics related to forensic ballistics and explosives. His area of research revolves around case-oriented practical problems and the development of innovative techniques. He has added new dimensions in the little-known and unsolvable area of illegally made firearms. He has published several papers in India and abroad. Besides being invited to talk in forensic institutes, seminars and workshops, Dr Sinha has been actively engaged in conferences in varied including chairman/co-chairman of scientific sessions.

Dr Sinha is the author of *Forensic Investigation of Unusual Firearms: Ballistic and Medico-legal Evidence* (2014, reprinted 2021), which ranks among the bestselling forensic firearm and medico-legal evidence books. Dr Sinha was the editor of the forensic firearm category of the open directory project of Netscape. He also hosted a popular web page on forensic firearm and unusual forensic ballistics, which ranked among the top five forensic science sites.

Forewords

The reliability and validity of opinions on identifying firearms from fired bullets and cartridge cases has become controversial in the USA and, as such, has demanded immediate attention. Dr J. K. Sinha, an eminent forensic firearm expert, has in this book provided multifaceted, demonstrative explanations and clarifications. The extraordinary characteristics of his book include the author's invaluable original, scientific, and practical explanations. His writing proves the scientific validity as to the uniqueness of identifying features of firearms in order to derive statistically significant opinions – and provide logical conclusions, dispelling unfounded controversies – as well as the *admissibility* of such experts' opinions to connect the firearm with the evidence bullet or cartridge case. *Forensic Firearms in Criminal Trials: Legal, Investigative, and Scientific Aspects* is an important landmark and an invaluable contribution to improving the investigation of shooting crimes to effectively utilize forensic science.

I strongly recommend this book as a handy reference for juries, investigators, lawyers, judges, and those adjudicating forensic firearm cases.

Professor (Dr) R.M. Sharma, Advisor (Forensics), National University of Law, Patiala, Former Dean, Faculty of Physical Sciences, Punjabi University, India

I am writing to recommend a comprehensive and insightful book that I believe would be invaluable for anyone involved in criminal law, particularly those dealing with cases involving firearms. The book is titled *Firearms in Criminal Trials: Legal, Investigative, and Scientific Aspects* authored by Dr J. K. Sinha who is a well-known senior forensic ballistic expert.

This book provides a thorough examination of the legal and forensic aspects related to examination of firearms and ammunition in criminal trials. It covers a wide range of topics, including but not limited to the legal framework surrounding the use of firearms in criminal cases, covering relevant statutes, case law, and legal precedents. It is an excellent resource for attorneys, judges, and legal scholars seeking a deeper understanding of the legal landscape. A significant portion of the book is dedicated to the forensic aspects of firearm evidence. It delves into the science behind ballistics, gunshot residue analysis, and other forensic techniques essential for understanding and presenting evidence in court. The author provides practical insights into presenting expert testimony related to firearms. This section is particularly helpful for attorneys who need to navigate the complexities of introducing and challenging firearm-related evidence during trials.

In the spirit of advancing our collective understanding of forensic firearms examination, I commend Dr Sinha for his scholarly contribution to the field. I am sure this book inspires a new generation of forensic scientists and legal professionals, fostering a commitment to excellence and unwavering dedication to the pursuit of justice.

Dr S. K. Jain, Chief Forensic Scientist,
Directorate of Forensic Science Services, MHA, India

Dr J.K. Sinha, an acclaimed forensic ballistics expert, presents a well-structured, valuable step-by-step guide for the investigation of visual and indirect evidence of physical clues in criminal cases involving firearms. Dr Sinha offers vivid explanations of the utility of the science of forensic ballistics which will help the investigating police officers to achieve a successful outcome in the judicial decision of the criminal trial. I recommend this book as a valuable reference for investigating police officers, prosecutors, enforcement agencies, lawyers, and all other professionals associated with criminal trials.

Dr Narinder Bhargav, IPS, Deputy Inspector General of Police,
Border Range, Amritsar, Punjab, India

Acknowledgments

I wish to express my sincere thanks to Prof. R. M. Sharma, Advisor (Forensic) at the National University of Law, Punjab, India; Dr. S. K. Jain, Chief Forensic Scientist for the Government of India; and Dr. Narinder Bhargav, IPS, Deputy Inspector General of Police, for writing their recommendations for the book and rating it as a timely informative book on the subject.

Special thanks to Mark Listewnik, my Commissioning Editor, for being extremely patient as well as for providing valuable suggestions and incisive reviews and helping at appropriate times to move the process of publishing this book forward. Thanks to Ella Halstead, Cathy Hurren and copyeditor, Katherine Laidler, for providing a thorough editorial check in the preparation of the final print of this book.

Thanks to my family for supporting me through the writing of this book, including going through multiple versions of the manuscript, which became very difficult at one point in time due to the Covid-19 pandemic and the changing scenario of discarding firearm identification.

PART I

Legal aspects in criminal trials involving firearms

1

Introduction to evidence in criminal trials involving firearms

A brief review

Evidence in criminal trials is the building block of the criminal justice system. It constitutes both direct and indirect evidence, where direct evidence is based on a statement of facts witnessing the criminal incident and indirect evidence is based on inferences – scientific or otherwise – drawn from circumstantial connection of the accused and the victim to the criminal incident. Both direct evidence and indirect evidence are relevant evidence that forms the basis for the jury and the courts to conclude whether the accused has committed the alleged crime. It solely depends upon the evidence management of the prosecution and the defendant to prove or disprove the facts produced before the trial court. Although details of evidence management are out of the purview of the present work, a brief review of managing gunfire evidence has been incorporated wherever necessary for the elucidation of the text in hand.

The most relevant direct evidence in shooting trials is the oral testimony of a witness or someone who has personal knowledge of the occurrence of the incident. The eyewitness statement is purported to be a true statement of observations of the criminal incident of gunfire and does not require any reasoning to prove the assertion. It therefore forms the primary basis for the trial against the suspect. The suspect, as per prevalent law, is innocent unless proven guilty, and to prove guilt, the onus lies on the enforcement agency.

DOI: 10.4324/9781351023863-2

The eyewitness testimony during the criminal trial is of paramount importance under the present legal system. It is often misused and at times misleading due to apparent drawbacks such as:

- The witness may be influenced by the suggestions of interested parties during the criminal trial.
- The witness may not recollect the shooting incident clearly if it occurred quickly and the witness was under stress.
- The witness may not remember the incident if the criminal trial commences after a considerable time lapse.
- An older witness may not record the incident accurately due to deteriorating sensory organs.
- The witness may lie for personal gain.
- The witness may be a tutored fake witness.

Such an eyewitness may impair justice. Besides probing the truthfulness of ocular witnesses, it becomes essential for an investigator to search for additional evidence to establish a linkage of the crime with the criminal. This calls for the search for indirect evidence that establishes the circumstantial connection of the accused and the victim to the criminal incident.

The most important indirect evidence is usually derived from the scientific analysis of physical exhibits that are related to the criminal incidents of gunfire. The court generally attributes high probative value to scientific evidence because the court can see and examine the physical exhibits, and so also can evaluate the expert opinion for deriving a judicious decision in the case. A variety of scientific evidence that employs traditional and modern instrumental and computer-generated analysis is placed before the present-day court. The court examines the relevancy and reliability of the scientific evidence.

The court allows the scientific evidence:

- *If the subject matter is outside the common knowledge and experience and is such that the science involved is highly specialized and only a recognized expert can provide necessary clarification and opinion on issues related to the commission of the crime.* The issues that are confronted during the criminal trial involving firearms indeed relate to the subject matter of the specialized field of forensic ballistics. Only an expert who specializes in the

field is competent to form an opinion and provide clarification related to the criminal incident of gunfire. The testimony of a firearm expert is often considered necessary and proves helpful in the judicious decision of gunfire cases.
- *If the expert's opinion and testimony are permissible under the law of evidence of the land.* The enacted worldwide evidence law provides legal provisions to allow the testimony of the expert's opinion with or without riders.
- *If the expert's opinion is reliable and demonstrable.*

It is not a simple proposition. It needs a brief discussion.

The science of forensic ballistics provides valuable clues to evaluate various gunfire-related issues such as firearm–ammunition linkage, identification of the firer, range of fire, whether suicide or homicide, accidental fire or murder, time of fire, etc.

The opinion of the expert that is of greatest concern in gunfire crimes is to establish the linkage of the seized fired ammunition with the suspected firearm. The moot question is, therefore, to ascertain whether such an opinion is reliable and demonstrable.

Among the early researchers, Colonel Calvin Godard was a pioneer whose identification skills were used not only for identifying firearms from fired bullets and cartridge cases but also for the uniqueness of consecutively manufactured and different parts of a barrel.

It was Godard who linked bullets from the crime scene with one of the assailant's firearms in the famous St Valentine's Day Massacre in 1929 when the assailants disguised themselves as police officers and shot seven of their rivals dead. This introduced millions of people to Godard, his invention of the comparison microscope and, above all, his ability to identify firearms from fired ammunition.

While discussing the details of successful identification, the court in the case of *Evans v. Commonwealth* (1929) held:

> We see no reason to quote further from this evidence, except to say that Major Goddard was permitted to make tests with other pistols of the same make, and was given shells that had been fired from the defendant's pistol and from other pistols, and he was able to identify the pistols from which they had been fired by an examination of the shells; these shells having been previously marked for the purpose of testing his identification.

Besides firearm–cartridge linkage, Godard also demonstrated before the court that no two barrels are alike to the extent that a barrel, even after finishing the process of rifling, if cut into two pieces to make two pistols, would imprint distinctly different identifying marks on their fired bullets that differentiate the pistol made from the rear part of the barrel from the pistol made from the front part of the barrel. The bullets from the pistols were also previously marked for the purpose of testing the expert's skill.

The results of these achievements in the field of forensic firearm identification led to the following significant conclusions:

- It proved the testability and reliability of the science of forensic firearm identification that outlines an important conclusive observation that every firearm bears characteristic identifying features, which differentiate one from the other even when they are of the same make and calibre.
- The methodology employed to differentiate between the identifying features of the rear and front parts of the same barrel is based on scientific principles and not on intuition and feelings.
- A competent examiner can differentiate the identifying features of one firearm from another and can provide a zero-error opinion by examining and comparing their fired ammunition.

It is pertinent to mention that as these observations were the outcome of the expert's practical demonstration, this resulted in their worldwide acceptance for many decades and they are still in vogue in most countries worldwide.

Over time, advancements in innovative scientific methodologies and the changing modus operandi of criminals have also triggered changes in the laws of evidence and the admissibility of expert evidence. There have been subsequent court rulings as well. Whereas the enacted law of evidence that outlines the criteria of specialized knowledge, education, training, experience, and skill to qualify as an expert is generally similar worldwide, it is the admissibility of the opinion and testimony that weighs most in making changes in the rule of evidence or court rulings from time to time and from one country to another.

The changes made in the rule of evidence, especially in the United States of America and India, have significantly influenced the admissibility of forensic evidence in general and firearm evidence in particular. The prevailing evidence laws in India empower the court to admit reports of certain government scientific experts as evidence, without their testimony, by virtue of the posts that they hold in forensic science laboratories and other allied government institutions engaged in forensic work. Contrarily, in the USA, in addition to the prevailing evidence rules, the federal court, in the case of *Daubert v. Merrell Pharmaceuticals, Inc* (1993) outlined additional stringent criteria for the admissibility of forensic evidence in criminal trials – popularly known as the Daubert standard, detailed in Chapter 2 on the admissibility of expert evidence in the USA. However, for elucidation, the consequential issues that need to be addressed in the prevailing criminal justice system have been briefly incorporated here as well.

Consequent on the court's directives of enforcing stringent criteria, experts have been confronted with a variety of issues on firearm–ammunition linkage such as the validity of the uniqueness of identifying features of firearms, non-scientific subjective methodology, testability and reliability, the unknown potential rate of error, unknown statistical certainty and unsatisfactory statistical proficiency tests. The expert's clarification and reasoning during their testimony on these issues were often considered unsatisfactory and treated as untenable by various courts. This posed big hurdles in accepting expert opinions on identifying firearms from fired ammunition. In the absence of known plausible reasons, the experts also conceded when confronted during cross-examination. This has resulted in the discarding of expert opinion and the emergence of a big question mark on the scientific validity of opinion on firearm–ammunition linkage.

The reports of various law schools, scientific forums of the USA such as NAS/NIST, related scientific articles published in peer-reviewed journals, etc., also broadly endorsed the observations of various courts. Enforcement agencies also took cognizance of the inability of the expert to explain and clarify the issues relating to their opinion on firearm–ammunition linkage and the courts' view thereupon for the rejection of the expert's opinion. In view of these, the Department of Justice issued guidelines for a government examiner on the qualification and limitation of the forensic firearm discipline, imposing strict restrictions on dos and don'ts that a ballistics expert has to follow while framing an opinion and during deposition in court. These are detailed in Chapter 2. A critical reading of one of the provisos – "an examiner shall not assert that two tool marks originated from the same source to the exclusion of all other sources" – implies that its application may negate even a positive firearm–empty linkage to the extent that the possibility of the firing of the empty from another source cannot be excluded and an alternate negative opinion cannot be ruled out; this is also implied to be true for the fired bullets.

In view of the above, this situation will continue to prevail until the objections/discrepancies are sorted out in rejecting experts' opinion, as observed by various courts, consequent on Dauber's criteria. As these issues are virtually the legal requirement for accepting an opinion on the identification of a firearm from fired ammunition, they assume great significance. This book provides a plausible scientific explanation and necessary clarifications by way of illustrative examples of simple scientific and everyday analogies on all such issues that have remained unanswered and disputed. These are discussed in detail in Part I of the book entitled "Legal Aspects in Criminal Trials Involving Firearms."

Part II deals with the investigative aspect of crime. It is well known that scientific evidence in criminal incidents of gunfire is mainly dependent on the physical evidence related to the firearms and ammunition that have been used in the commission of the crime and the target that has been hit. This calls upon the investigators to search and seize physical clues related to gunfire crime for scientific examination and forensic opinion for the proper presentation of the case in the criminal trial. This necessitates that the investigators must have requisite forensic knowledge of the probable opinion on the seized physical clues that can be had from ballistic experts to corroborate, prove or disprove the guilt of the accused. This does not necessarily mean that investigators need to be forensic firearm experts as well. What forensic knowledge needs most for the investigation of gunfire crime is dealt with in detail in the second part of the book, which includes a basic understanding of the general make-up of firearms and ammunition, the evidentiary values of commonly used firearms, fired empties, fired projectiles (bullets, pellets, wads), investigative leads and, above all, a number of dos and don'ts that will not only help the investigator to conduct an appropriate and scientifically effective investigation but also provide a ready reckoner for the defense to cross-examine. Part II is entitled "Investigative Aspects in Criminal Trials Involving Firearms."

Part III deals with the scientific aspects of crime involving firearms. Most of the issues relating to the science of forensic ballistics have been dealt with in the preceding sections in varied contexts which include plausible solutions to the disputed issues on firearm–ammunition linkage. This section deals with the important issue of minimizing errors, which experts need to address during the examination and forming of opinion in order to achieve an error-free opinion.

The concluding chapter of the book deals with the relative merits and demerits of eyewitness and scientific evidence.

2
Admissibility of Ballistics Expert Evidence in Criminal Trials in the United States

The admissibility of ballistics expert evidence in the USA centres around the prevailing Federal Rule of Evidence 702, two monumental court judgments popularly known as the Frye and Daubert standards, and guidelines enforced by the Department of Justice for uniformity of testimony and reports of government ballistic experts. Their implications in the present scenario of criminal justice system are varied and need further discussion.

2.1 Frye standard

About a century ago, the criteria of admissibility of scientific evidence in criminal trials was laid down in the case *Frye v. United States* (1923) popularly known as the Frye standard. It emphasized that the opinion of an expert is admissible if it is based on scientific principles and techniques that are accepted in the scientific community of that field.

While discussing the admissibility of scientific evidence, the court had held:

> while the courts will go a long way in admitting expert testimony deduced from a well-recognized scientific principle or discovery, the thing from which the deduction is made must be sufficiently established to have gained general acceptance in the particular field in which it belongs.

DOI: 10.4324/9781351023863-3

2.2 Federal Rule of Evidence 702

In 1975, the Federal Rule of Evidence 702 was enacted in the United States of America which reads:

> A witness who is qualified as an expert by knowledge, skill, experience, training, or education may testify in the form of an opinion or otherwise if…
>
> (a) the expert's scientific, technical, or other specialized knowledge will help the trier of fact to understand the evidence or to determine a fact in issue;
> (b) the testimony is based on sufficient facts or data;
> (c) the testimony is the product of reliable principles and methods; and
> (d) the expert's opinion reflects a reliable application of the principles and methods to the facts of the case.

These specific criteria of sufficient data, reliability and methodology have been enacted as prerequisite riders for admissibility of expert opinion and testimony in trial courts. It seems, despite specific provisions under Federal Rule 702, that the Frye test of the admissibility of an expert's opinion and testimony prevailed until it was overruled by a federal court decision in 1993, popularly known as Daubert standard.

2.3 Daubert standard

A new standard of admissibility of expert evidence emerged in the case *Daubert v. Merrell Dow Pharmaceuticals Inc.* (1993). The federal court (Supreme Court of the USA) outlined stringent criteria in addition to the prevailing evidence rules. While discussing the proviso of prevailing Evidence Rule 702, the federal court issued directives for the trial court. In this respect, the court held:

> General acceptance is not a necessary precondition to the admissibility of scientific evidence under the Federal Rules of Evidence, but the Rules of Evidence especially Rule 702 do assign to the trial judge the task of ensuring that an expert's testimony both rests on a reliable foundation and is relevant to the task at hand. Pertinent evidence based on scientifically valid principles will satisfy those demands.

The directive forms the basic premise of the proviso of the Evidence Rule 702. It emphasizes that the trial judge must exercise the powers assigned under the Evidence Rule to make a decision on the admissibility of an expert's evidence on the basis of prerequisite criteria of data, reliability and methodology. This aspect of the court's ruling very often resulted in challenging the admissibility of the testimony of the expert who is called upon to appear before the court to prove the report that had been submitted on firearm–ammunition linkage.

The other significant premise of the court's ruling relates to enforcing of the outlined additional criteria for judicious outcome of the scientific evidence placed during the trial. In this context, the court held:

> whether a theory or technique is scientific knowledge that will assist the trier of fact will be whether it can be (and has been) tested [...]
>
> whether the theory or technique has been subjected to peer review and publication. [...] [I]n the case of a particular scientific technique, the court ordinarily should consider the known or potential rate of error [...]
>
> Finally, 'general acceptance' can yet have a bearing on the inquiry. [...]
>
> Widespread acceptance can be an important factor in ruling particular evidence admissible, and 'a known technique that has been able to attract only minimal support within the community' [...]
>
> may properly be viewed with skepticism.

Consequent upon the U.S federal court directives of enforcing stringent criteria for admissibility of expert evidence, the prevailing defence trend, in the recent past, has been to seek a Daubert motion. The experts have been accordingly confronted with a variety of issues that are directly or indirectly related to the court rulings, such as the validity of the uniqueness of identifying features of firearms, subjective methodology, unknown potential error rate and unknown statistical certainty. Reasons and clarifications put forward by experts on most of these issues were treated as untenable by various courts and have remained unanswered to date. In the absence of plausible reasoning, experts have also conceded to testify against the fundamental principles of forensic firearm identification. This has resulted in the discarding of experts' opinion especially on firearm–ammunition linkage – an important link to connect the crime with the criminal weapon. Significant issues and discrepancies that have led to the discarding of the ballistics experts' opinion and testimony are worth mentioning. They are:

- The theory of uniqueness is not proven.
- The expert could only describe ways in which casings were similar but not that the casings came from specific weapon to the exclusion of every other firearm in the world.
- While the underlying principles behind firearm identification may be scientifically valid, scientific methodology is not reliable, which will permit the expert to testify that an empty or a bullet and a particular firearm are linked with an absolute certainty.
- The methodology is based on the examiner's training and experience, and it remains for the examiner to determine the modicum of proof necessary to arrive at a definite opinion. The examiner's conclusion is a subjective judgment. In this sense, firearm identification is more of an art than a science.

The reports of scientific forums such as National Academy of Sciences/ National Institute of Standard and Technology (NAST/NIST) of the United States of America, projects of various law schools on the prevailing ballistic evidence, and the Association of Firearms and Tool Mark Examiners broadly endorsed the court's observations on the limitations of the validity of the science of firearm identification. The enforcement agencies also took cognizance of the experts' inability to explain and clarify issues related to the Daubert standard and consequential court's observations in rejecting the ballistic report especially on firearm–ammunition linkage. This resulted in the issuance of Department of Justice guidelines on the qualification and limitation of forensic firearms discipline examinations.

2.3.1 Department of Justice guidelines for government examiners

The relevant extracts of the Department of Justice guidelines for department examiners (2020) are reproduced below.

> Uniform Language for Testimony and Reports is a quality assurance measure designed to standardize the expression of appropriate

consensus language for use by Department examiners in their reports and testimony. A conclusion provided during testimony or in a report is ultimately an examiner's decision and is not based on a statistically derived or verified measurement or comparison to all other firearms or tool-marks. Therefore, an examiner shall not:

i) assert that a "source identification" or a "source exclusion" conclusion is based on the "uniqueness" of an item of evidence.
ii) use the terms "individualize" or "individualization" when describing a source conclusion.
iii) assert that two tool-marks originated from the same source to the exclusion of all other sources.
iv) An examiner shall not assert that examinations conducted in the forensic firearms/tool-marks discipline are infallible or have a zero-error rate.
v) An examiner shall not provide a conclusion that includes a statistical or numerical degree of probability except when based on relevant and appropriate data.
vi) An examiner shall not assert that two tool-marks originated from the same source with absolute or 100% certainty or use the expressions "reasonable degree of scientific certainty," "reasonable scientific certainty," or similar assertions of reasonable certainty in either reports or testimony unless required to do so by a judge or applicable law.

In view of the above deliberations, it is evident that this situation will continue to prevail until plausible explanations on the aforementioned objections/discrepancies in accepting the firearm evidence are sorted out. Therefore, it is considered necessary to evaluate the possibility of providing plausible solutions to all such issues that remain disputed. The foremost issue that needs to be addressed is the uniqueness of identifying features of a firearm.

2.4 Scientific validity of uniqueness of identifying features of a firearm

For an objective assessment of the factors that establish the uniqueness of identifying features of a firearm, it is fruitful to explain by way of simple examples. The following illustration gives a brief idea of the uniqueness of identifying features of firearms.

2.4.1 Law of uniqueness of nature

It is a well-known law of nature that no two objects, whether God- or human-made/manufactured, are identical. Even so-called identical twins are not truly identical. Uniqueness does exist that differentiates one from the other. An experienced and trained eye such as that of a parent can easily identify the uniqueness between twins.

Based on this law of nature, it is an undisputed truth that every person has unique identifying features which differentiate one from another. This assumption is universally accepted even for a witness appearing in court. It has a legal validity as well. As this premise has legal validity, it cannot be just a universal belief. The simplest approach to prove the assumption would be to examine the unique identifying features of the entire world population to verify whether one person is duplicated in any other. But it is virtually an impossible task to physically examine billions of people in the world population to achieve one hundred percent mathematical certainty. Does it necessarily mean that until physically verified, the identity of a witness on the basis of identifying features can lead to only one possible conclusion that it is more likely than not the same person appearing as witness but not to the extent of the exclusion of the entire world population? There cannot be any plausible answer other than "No" and it is neither customary nor necessary to verify the identifying features of every person of the entire world population to prove that there is no other person of the same identifying features as that of the witness appearing in the court, living or dead.

This uniqueness of the law of nature is also true for firearms that are manufactured or human-made. Even the so-called "smooth-bore barrel" manufactured by employing precision instruments is not truly smooth. When viewed under a microscope, the interior of a shining smooth-bore barrel shows minute imperfections in the form of elevations and depressions of variable heights and depths. They are created during various manufacturing processes of the barrel and are randomly distributed from the rear to the front end of the barrel – an experimentally proven scientific truth. Subsequent wear and tear, corrosion and erosion, accidental marks during usage, etc. make the variation in the resultant random imperfections more pronounced and adds uniqueness in identifying features of the firearm. They are bound to vary from one barrel to another, or one make and model to another, and even between the rear and front parts of the same barrel; randomly created imperfections can therefore truly act as unique identifying features of the firearm. These experimental observations clearly reveal that the identifying features of every smooth-bore/rifled barrel are unique.

2.4.2 Significance of tolerance limits in manufacturing processes

It is well known that no two objects can be manufactured with identical dimensions, even when working on the same assembly line; there exist variations in the resultant dimensions of consecutively manufactured objects, mainly because of the manufacturing limits of tolerance within which each dimension such as length, breadth, height, gradient, radius, circumference and thickness has to be made. There will always exist a variation, however minute it may be, between one and the other due to limits of tolerance in the manufacturing process. The fact is that even for the manufacture of a precise dimension of a depth of groove of rifled barrels, the assigning of a manufacturing limit of variation in its dimension is needed despite sophisticated modern computerized manufacturing instrumental techniques. The dimensional variation limits may be as small as a few thousandths of an inch, such as, +/– .0002″. Such is the case with the width of the grooves, angle of rifling, land width, rifle bore diameter, etc. This results in variation in the resultant dimensions of the rifling parameters of consecutively manufactured rifled barrels. There exist variations even between the grooves of the same barrel, although these may be minute. The bore of consecutively manufactured barrels and other parts of the firearm such as the breech, firing pin and chamber will always show some variation.

The aforesaid deliberation provides a plausible explanation that no two objects whether God- or human-made are identical and that the identifying features of every smooth bore/rifled barrel are unique.

Associated with the uniqueness of identifying features of a firearm, there is another important issue to prove that it is not duplicated in any other firearm. Although this has been experimentally verified by various scientists in the past, the number of such experiments has obviously been limited. Is it now necessary to examine the entire world's firearm population to verify their unique identifying features, as envisaged in the present prevailing observations and directives? Even if considered necessary, would it be possible to do so? Obviously not, as there are innumerable firearms that would need to be examined for the purpose, and it is virtually impossible to achieve one hundred percent mathematical certainty by physical verification. Under the circumstances, would it mean that unless so physically verified, there cannot be any plausible conclusion other than "it is only likely to be the one but not to the extent of excluding every other firearm existing in the world"? There does not appear any scientific basis to conclude so.

The question remains whether there exists a recourse other than one hundred percent physical verification of millions of data points to prove an assumption or hypothesis. Such a situation also arises in most of the major findings in science. A well-known scientific recourse is the measure of statistical significance to achieve statistical certainty instead of one hundred percent mathematical certainty, which is neither feasible to achieve nor a scientific requirement in such a population of data. This calls for evaluation of statistical significance for assessing the statistical certainty of identifying features of firearm.

2.4.3 Statistical certainty of unique identifying features of firearm

The measure of statistical significance is the probable value of occurrence denoted by a number expressed in lower-case Greek letter sigma. It represents the amount of variability in a given set of data. One sigma corresponds to about 84.11% certainty, two sigma to 97.73%, three sigma to 99.87%, five sigma to 99.9999% and so on. The corresponding p-value or the chance of faulty observation is only about 0.00001% for five sigma – i.e. about 1 in 3.5 million, about one in half a billion for six sigma, about one in 10 billion for seven sigma and so on. The higher the sigma value, the lower the p-value, which is more and more towards approaching certainty. The following illustration provides a brief idea about its worldwide acceptance in the scientific community.

In 2012, the scientists at CERN declared the discovery of the Higgs boson particle as approaching five-sigma certainty. Obviously, five sigma was considered to be the threshold for an observation to be labelled as a scientific discovery in particle physics of the kind involving millions of data points. This was talked about extensively in the media as a monumental discovery, coined "God's particle". This clearly signifies that an appropriate sigma or p-value achieved in particle physics experimentations provided a certain criterion for declaring a scientific discovery to be true. Undoubtedly, this criterion had a worldwide acceptance in the scientific community. In 2015, CERN is believed to have announced that the observation of Higgs boson had approached seven-sigma certainty, signifying that there is only a 0.00000000001% (i.e. about one in 10 billion) chance of uncertainty that the Higgs particle was found. It is thus apparent that to prove a hypothesis to be a scientific truth, when the data is in millions or billions, one needs to establish a statistical certainty just in terms of sigma(s) and not an absolute one hundred percent mathematical certainty.

This criterion of assessing statistical certainty by the threshold value of sigma can now conveniently be utilized for declaring a proposition or hypothesis to be a scientifically proven reality in the field of forensic ballistics as well – a true scientific approach to prove the fundamental hypothesis that every barrel bears characteristic identifying features which are not duplicatable even in firearms of the same make and calibre. The pertinent question is what constitutes the identifying features of a firearm and how can one find the same. It has already been explained above that randomly created imperfections inside the barrel represent the identifying features of the firearm. It remains to be explored how to find the identifying features of a firearm. The methodology adopted is discussed in detail below.

A bullet, during its travel inside the bore, makes sliding contacts with the imperfections of the barrel which result in the creation of striations on its surface. When striations are examined and compared side by side under a comparison microscope, they show matching points in some of the striations that are repeated on each of the bullets fired from the same firearm. The number of striations that match can also be counted. As the number of matching striations represents specific imperfections of the barrel that caused similar striations repeatedly on every fired bullet, the number of matching striations can also act as the number of identifying features of the firearm. Thus, to ascertain the identifying features of the firearm, one needs to find out only the number of matching striations among the test bullets fired from that firearm.

Once the number of matching striations is known, it becomes easier to find the threshold sigma or p-value that proves or disproves the hypothesis that "every barrel bears characteristic identifying marks" to be a statistical certainty. Therefore, only the number of matching striations that have been found on bullets fired from the same firearm needs to be ascertained, which would represent the number of identifying features of the firearm.

It is well known to experts in the field that there are usually 10–12 matching striations even on a small part of fired test bullets that are simultaneously viewed under the comparison microscope. As comparison is not limited to just one or two specific positions but all along 360 degrees, the resultant number of matching striations is invariably in multiples of tens and sometimes even in hundreds.

It is obvious that one would expect the possibility of the recurrence of imperfections in the same lot of manufactured firearms. Therefore, for a meaningful assessment of the threshold of the sigma or p-value, it is desirable that a liberal view of many probable recurrences in a particular lot of manufactured firearms is assumed for the study. Keeping this in mind, if one of the identifying features of a firearm recurs in as many as 2,000 firearms out of a manufactured lot of 200,000, then the probability of such a recurrence will be 2,000/200,000 or .01. Assuming that ten such identifying features or imperfections recur at exactly the same positions in another barrel of a firearm, then the probability of such an integrated recurrence would be the continued product of the probability of .01, i.e., ten times – one for each of the ten recurrences. This would mean a p-value of .00000000001, which corresponds to a probability of one in 10 billion. This outnumbers many times the total number of 200,000 manufactured firearms of the same lot and make under the study, therefore rendering such a duplication as virtually non-existent and non-viable. This p-value of .0000000001%, a one-in-ten-billion chance of recurrence, corresponds to an extremely high degree of seven sigma of statistical certainty as per the norms explained above. This incidentally is even more stringent than was achieved in particle physics experiments such as that at CERN, and thus leads to an obvious conclusion that the identifying marks of a firearm are not duplicated in another even of the same make and lot, and therefore the proposition that "every barrel bears characteristic identifying marks" is based on a well-recognized scientific principle of statistical certainty. It can very well be assessed that if the number of matching striations is in a multiple of tens or more, then the probability of recurrence will be so low that it may outnumber by many times the total population of the world's firearms.

The same is true for identifying marks on fired empty shells. As expected, random imperfections are also created on various parts of the firearm during their manufacturing and finishing processes. These imperfections are usually in the form of lines, curves, arches, dots, etc. of varied shapes and sizes, with irregular elevations and depressions. These imperfections create static and/or sliding marks on empty shells fired from the firearm that come in contact with the parts of the firearm during firing, such as the firing pin, breech face, chamber, extractor and ejector. The relative distribution of these marks on each of these parts of the firearm provides the necessary matching of repeated marks that represent the identifying features of the firearm. The number of matching points on each of the parts is often more than 8–10, which corresponds to a similar p-value and sigma derivative range as that of bullet examination and conclusion of 6–7 sigma statistical certainty. Achieving statistical certainty of 6–7 sigma is the threshold for the matching of identifying marks for firearm–ammunition linkage.

This provides plausible scientific clarification for testifying to being certain of the match in terms of achieving 6–7 sigma of statistical certainty.

2.4.4 Scientific validity of methodology adopted for identifying firearm from fired ammunition

The scientifically valid procedure of identifying individual features of the firearm from fired bullets and empty shells, and then establishing their linkage to the suspect firearm, now becomes a simple task. The first step is to identify individual features of the suspect firearm. To do so, as explained above, test cartridges are fired from the suspect firearm to ascertain marks that are repeated on each of its fired bullets and empty shells. A side-by-side examination and comparison under a comparison microscope leads to the identification of the repeated marks present on the test-fired bullets and empty shells which identify the individual features of the firearm. Having known the marks that match, the next step is to compare those marks with the marks on the seized fired bullets and empty shells primarily to ascertain whether a similar match exists between the test and the seized bullets or empty shells. A similar match between the two would establish the linkage of the seized bullets or empty shells with the suspect firearm and eliminate any other firearm, even one of same make and model.

Now, it needs to be established that the procedure adopted for identifying firearms from fired ammunitions is verifiable, repeatable and reliable – an important aspect of forensic firearm identification (and of proving a scientific postulate). It assumes great legal significance if the testability and reliability can be demonstrated before the court. It will help in ensuring due probative value to the adopted procedure for accepting the expert's opinion with greater certainty.

2.4.5 Testability and reliability of the methodology for identifying firearm from fired ammunition

Various researchers in the field have experimented with consecutively manufactured rifled barrels to test the uniqueness and reliability of the methodology adopted for identifying a firearm from fired ammunition. An exhaustive list of researchers was provided by Hamby et al. in their 2009 paper, "The identification of bullets fired from10 consecutively rifled 9mm Ruger pistol barrels: a research project involving 507 participants from 20 countries."

Even at the infancy stage of the recognition of the field of forensic ballistics, the uniqueness of consecutively manufactured rifled barrels and the reliability of the identifying procedure had been the core issue for establishing the science of forensic firearm identification.

Colonel Godard experimented with rifled barrels which were consecutively manufactured with the same cutter. He was able to differentiate between the bullets fired from the consecutively manufactured rifled barrels.

In 1930, in the U.S Government arsenal, a rifled barrel was cut into six pieces to form six barrels. A bullet was fired from each of the six barrels and scribed with a secret marking. Colonel Godard was given the fired bullets and the six barrels for identification. He was able to correctly match each of the rifled barrels that fired the specific bullets.

In the present context, it is worthwhile to recapitulate the demonstration during the criminal trial in the case *Evans vs. Commonwealth* (1929), wherein Colonel Godard demonstrated the reliability of the methodology for the linkage of fired bullets and empty shells with the questioned firearm. To test the scientific validity and the skill of the expert, empties fired from firearms of the same make and calibre were secretly marked. Likewise, bullets were also marked secretly that were fired from a pair of pistols, each fixed with a half cut of one single barrel, one having the rear part and the other, the front. The ballistic expert was required to establish linkage of each of the pistols with the secretly marked bullets and also to identify each of the firearms of the same make with the secretly marked specific empty shells. While discussing the objections of the defending attorney and the demonstrative evidence of the expert, the court held:

> [T]he witness stated it was the practice of one factory in making pistol barrels to make them in double lengths, to rifle them and finish them before they are cut in two, *and the defendant argues* that therefore these two barrels will be made exactly alike, and that hence the witness' statement that no two barrels were exactly alike is untrue; but he overlooks the fact that Goddard testified that he had three bars of steel so bored and finished, thus making six barrels, that two shots were fired from each of the six barrels, that they were marked for the purpose of testing his skill, and that he had then taken these pistols, and, by firing them, recovering the balls, and comparing them with the twelve balls given him, he was able to say from which of the six barrels they had been fired. That disposes of that objection.
>
> [...] We see no reasons to quote further from this evidence, except to say that Major Goddard was permitted to make tests with other pistols of the same make, and was given shells that had been fired from the defendant's pistol and from other pistols, and he was able to identify the pistols from which they had been fired by an examination of the shells; these shells having been previously marked for the purpose of testing his identification.

This demonstration proved the testability and reliability of

(a) the procedure adopted for establishing the linkage of fired empty shells and bullets with the firearm
(b) the scientific principle that led to the statement that no two barrels are alike to the extent that a barrel, even after finishing the process of rifling, if cut into two pieces to make two pistols, would imprint distinctly different identifying marks on their fired bullets that differentiates one pistol from the other

(c) the unique identifying features of firearms that differentiates one from the other even of same make and calibre.

These scientific findings coupled with the above-mentioned theoretical and practical deliberation on uniqueness and high degree of statistical certainty makes forensic firearm identification a scientific reality which is reliable and verifiable. Of course, the obvious rider is that the examiner must be a skilled person having the requisite expertise in the field of forensic ballistics. Regardless, post Daubert's case court ruling, the ballistic experts, especially in US, usually prefer not to claim that ballistics is a science and do not assert that the conclusion drawn in establishing firearm–ammunition linkage to the exclusion of all other firearms is based on established scientific principles and statistical certainty.

Such a testimony would obviously contribute to the unfounded misconception that there is every possibility of error in the ballistic expert's report especially on the firearm–ammunition linkage.

2.5 Potential rate of error and element of subjectivity

Ballistics experts are often required to state the potential rate of error. Before assessing the same, it must be known what constitutes the rate of potential error in scientific experiments. The following illustration gives a brief idea of the same.

It is well known that school, college and university students are allowed a certain percentage of error in their results of scientific experiments to qualify in their practical examination. Despite experimental errors, the scientific technique employed to prove the theory stands correct and accepted as a reliable technique in the academic and scientific community. The error may be minimized if the experimenter has received adequate training in experimental setup, the procedure of experimentation, observations and their interpretation. The error may further be minimized if the experimenter has gained adequate experience of carrying out such experiments. A person having adequate training and experience can achieve far more accurate experimental results than those who are not trained and experienced, whether they possess adequate or inadequate knowledge about the scientific theory and principles involved. Those who have requisite training and experience without adequate scientific knowledge of the subject are better known as technicians rather than scientists. Such a person may not be able to clarify the intricacies of the scientific principles of the experiment under purview and to evaluate unforeseen complex problems therein for a successful outcome. This necessitates a qualified scientific person to be an essential and important parameter for achieving successful outcomes of a scientific experiment.

In view of the above, it is evident that the potential rate of error for any scientific experiment would vary according to how one is equipped with the parameters of knowledge, training, experience, qualifications and skill. The potential rate of error would be the highest when one does not possess the required proficiency in any of these. Contrarily, it would be at its minimum, or almost non-existent, when one is equipped with all the parameters equally well, a prerequisite criterion to qualify as an expert. Thus, it needs no emphasis that variation in the potential rate of error, whether maximum, minimum, or in between, does not change at any stage the field of science to a non-scientific field of art, and it is not the element of the subjectivity of bias, intuition or feelings but rather the expertise that matters in forming correct opinion. The rider, of course, is a competent expert.

It is also an established fact that there are certain scientific experiments that require the utmost precision. Even a minor error may affect the desired result adversely, such as an ICBM (inter-continental ballistic missile), the launching of satellite on a preassigned orbit, a concentrated laser surgery on a very small area, etc. In such cases, near-zero error is a must. It becomes binding that persons involved in the project must have adequate knowledge of the science as well as the scientific techniques, besides adequate experience and training in the field.

This is equally true in the field of forensic sciences. An insignificant error in the opinion on certain issues may considerably affect the judicious decision of a criminal trial. One such issue in the field of forensic ballistics, cited earlier, is the opinion on the linkage of empty and fired bullets with the suspect firearm which connects the criminal with the crime through the weapon of offence. As the life and liberty of the suspect in such cases hangs on the opinion of the ballistic expert, it must be devoid of any error. The potential rate of error should be virtually non-existent. This will necessitate an error-free interpretation of the scientific analysis of the experiments for forming an opinion on the linkage of seized fired bullets and empty shells with the suspect firearm.

Is it possible to achieve such a reliable opinion? This needs to be further explored.

2.6 Interpreting scientific analysis for achieving reliable opinion on firearm–ammunition linkage

A reliable opinion on firearm–ammunition linkage means a virtually zero-error opinion. This can be ensured only if the interpretation of scientific experiments for forming such an opinion is devoid of any error. It must be specific and unambiguous, which can aid the court to form a judicious and correct decision of the crime. The following illustrative example gives a brief idea of how to achieve this seeming difficult state.

Let us suppose that there are four photographs marked A, B, C and D. They are photographs of three persons: photographs A and B are well-focused, clear photographs of the same person at two distinct locations; photographs C and D are also well focused and clear photographs but are of two different persons. If a witness, an expert or otherwise, is called in the court to identify persons from the above photographs, it will not be difficult to state that A and B are photographs of the same person, while C and D are photographs of two different persons. A similar outcome can be expected from any other witness if confronted with the same set of photographs. This indicates that the test for differentiating one person from another from photographs bearing clear, well-focused, identifiable features is demonstrative and reliable.

The problem arises if the photographs of the aforesaid three people do not bear clear, identifying features. To elucidate further, let us now suppose that there is another set of photographs of the same three persons marked E, F and G. The photograph of person A or B is completely out of focus marked as E; the second person C is photographed in a very poor light without flash marked as F; and the third person D is photographed while running in heavy rain, marked as G. Under such a circumstance, if a witness, expert or otherwise, is called in the court to identify persons from the set of photographs marked E, F and G, it may neither be possible to identify nor to differentiate one from the other because of the lack of clear, identifying features. The only plausible opinion that one could expect in such a set of photographs would be that it is not possible to form any definite opinion despite the fact they are the photographs of the same three persons easily identifiable when confronted with the photographs marked A, B, C and D. It is, thus, evident that the opinion is based on whether the set bears clear/identifiable or blurred/non-identifiable individual features.

One is likely to arrive at a wrong conclusion if an attempt is made to identify the person from the blurred and hazy photographs, or if the witness is incompetent to make the right decision due to impaired vision, deteriorating age, mental instability, physical ailments, etc.

The illustrative example mentioned previously has similarities between the photographs of a person and that of the fired ammunition from a firearm. This comparison makes the science of forensic firearm identification easily understandable to even non-technical personal.

i) Just as identifying features are imprinted on the photographs of a person, the identifying features of a firearm are imprinted on its fired ammunition such as empties, bullets, pellets, etc.
ii) Just as identifying features in photographs of a person differentiates one from the other, the identifying features on the fired ammunition too differentiates one firearm from another.
iii) Just as identifying features may or may not be clearly imprinted on the photographs of a person, the identifying features of a firearm also may or may not be clearly imprinted on its fired ammunition.
iv) Just as it is possible to form a definite opinion only if the photograph bears identifiable individual features of the person, it is also so that a definite opinion is possible only if the fired ammunition bears identifiable individual features of the firearm.
v) Just as identifying people from their photographs is demonstrative and reliable, identification of firearms from their fired ammunition is similarly demonstrative and reliable, as has been explained earlier.
vi) Just as it is not possible to form an opinion in the absence of identifying features in the photographs of a person, it is also not possible to form an opinion in the absence of identifying features of the firearm on its fired ammunition.
vii) Just as it is not enough to have only a photograph of a person for identification, but it is also essential that the photograph

> must bear identifiable features of the person for forming a definite opinion, similarly it is also not enough to have only the ammunition fired from the firearm for identification, but it is also essential that the fired ammunition must carry clear and identifiable individual features of the firearm for forming a definite opinion, whether fired or not.

In view of the above deliberations, it is clear that the fired ammunition may or may not always carry sufficient identifiable features of the suspect firearm. If available and identifiable, it would be either similar or dissimilar. It needs to be known how to evaluate similar and dissimilar marks in order to form a definite opinion.

2.6.1 Similar and dissimilar marks and general perception

It is the similar and dissimilar marks on the evidence and test ammunition that lead to the formation of a definite opinion. It is worthwhile to discuss how similar and dissimilar marks are evaluated to form a definite positive or a negative opinion.

For a meaningful understanding of the difference between similar and dissimilar marks, let us take the example of the aforementioned well-focused photographic illustrations marked A and B of the same person at two distinct locations, one in the natural surroundings of a busy park and the other relaxing in a living room. On examination and comparison, one would observe that the only similar marks present on both photographs would be the identifying features of the person. All other marks/objects present on A would be entirely different and dissimilar compared to objects contained in B, being the surroundings of the park and the living room, respectively. The other relevant observation would be that despite dissimilarities between A and B outnumbering by many times the similar marks, *it is the similar marks of identifying features which lead one to infer that both A and B are photographs of the same person*. This is mainly due to the fact that neither the busy park nor the living room bears any identifying features of the person, and therefore they are extraneous marks which do not make any difference whether they are similar or dissimilar and by what quantum.

This analogy is comparable to photomicrographs of the identifying marks on evidence and test ammunitions and the extraneous marks present on them. It is the similar or dissimilar marks of identifying features of the firearm that will determine a definite positive or a definite negative opinion. The extraneous marks, dissimilar or otherwise, and their numbers present on the evidence and test ammunitions do not play any role in the identification of the firearm. It is not the number of similar or/and dissimilar marks in totality that leads to the formation of correct opinion.

General perception

In view of the above, it is evident that *the misconception that the matching of striations or other identifying marks on evidence and test must be totally identical without any dissimilarities, whether extraneous or otherwise, is incorrect.*

Thus, if the identifying features of the firearm are available and identifiable, it would lead to one of the following opinions:

- that the seized empty and/or fired bullet had been fired from the suspect firearm and not from any other firearm even of same make and bore; or
- the seized empty and/or fired bullet had not been fired from the suspect firearm.

Only such an opinion would establish the linkage or elimination of the suspect firearm with the seized fired ammunition.

Contrarily, if the fired ammunition does not carry sufficient identifying features, it would be possible neither to establish nor to eliminate the suspect firearm. The only plausible and correct opinion that can be formed in such cases is that:

- it is not possible to form definite opinion whether or not the seized empty or fired bullet had been fired from the suspect firearm due to insufficient or lack of identifying marks.

These deliberations reveal that it is the clarity of marks on fired ammunition that makes a difference in forming a positive or an inconclusive opinion – or a no-definite opinion. The truth is that even an expert who fires cartridges for test purposes may certify as an individual that all the test cartridges have been fired from the said firearm, but as an expert it may not be possible to certify that the test ammunition has been fired from the same firearm unless identifying marks are available on all to confirm so. In those cartridges bearing insufficient marks, even the expert must form a no-definite opinion instead of a positive opinion, despite the expert firing the ammunition from the same gun.

This clearly shows that the difference in the opinion (positive or no definite opinion) on cartridges fired from the same firearm is not because the science of firearm identification is fallible and unreliable, but it is only the presence or absence of identifying marks that makes the difference, which may vary from one round to the other because of variable factors such as pressure, hardness of the metal of the primer, etc.

However, it is equally true that one is liable to form a wrong opinion if an attempt is made to form a definite opinion (positive or negative) despite insufficient or lack of identifying marks. It must be borne in mind that an expert is a party neither to the prosecution nor to the defence; a scientific expert is a neutral witness assisting the court to establish the truth with his scientific opinion on firearm–ammunition linkage. The expert need not be overenthusiastic to form an opinion despite insufficient or lack of identifying marks. Obviously, such an expert would contribute to creating unfounded doubts about the testability and reliability of the science of firearm identification. Therefore, the most important rider for a zero-error opinion is the skill and expertise of the examiner who is trusted to form an opinion. It is therefore necessary to discuss details of the requisite criteria to be a competent ballistic expert, in the first place.

2.7 Identifying competent ballistic experts

The Federal Rule of Evidence 702 outlines essential criteria for a witness to testify as an expert and to qualify for forming an opinion on issues that are relevant to the crime. The relevant extract of the Federal Rule 702 states that "a witness who is qualified as an expert by knowledge, skill, experience, training or education may testify in the form of an opinion or otherwise." This forms the prerequisite criterion for the admissibility of expert's opinion in criminal trials involving firearms. However, the rule does not specify the requisite qualification, experience and training to qualify as ballistic experts. It is for the enforcement agencies to identify the appropriate minimum and desirable qualification, experience and training for government experts, in accordance with the law of evidence. This needs to be reviewed with changes in crime patterns, identification methodologies and the court's directives, if any. Therefore, it is obligatory on the part of the enforcement agencies to assess and enforce the quality and quantum of any of these criteria for necessary updating during changing times, especially for government experts.

In recent times, there have been unprecedented changes in crime pattern. The importance of positive opinion for conviction and negative opinion for acquittal, even in heinous crimes, is no secret to present-day criminals. Thus, to eliminate the firearm that was used in the crime, the licensee or the easily traceable owner attempts to destroy or tamper with the identifying parts of the firearm before the firearm is seized by enforcement agencies or surrendered. This poses varied problems in forming positive, negative, or inconclusive opinions for the expert and needs special skill to form the correct opinion.

To evade detection by firearm tracing such as IBIS, NIBIN, etc., the use of illegally manufactured or illegally procured firearms has increased greatly in recent times. These firearms often give rise to ambiguous marks that are misleading to unwary examiners. In such cases, one has to remain either non-committal or modify the known identification procedures to form an opinion. One also comes across instances where misleading similar or dissimilar marks are present on the fired cartridges and bullets such as extraneous marks, subclass marks, etc.

From the above deliberations, it is evident that the present era of forensic firearm identification is an one of frequent and unforeseen challenges in the evaluation of misleading and ambiguous exhibits in firearm cases. It is no longer confined to the routine application of basic principles of the matching of tool-marks by adopting known identification procedures for forming an opinion strictly in accordance with the prevailing manual, if any. It must be understood that the manual is only a valuable guide and not a foolproof ready reckoner for achieving success in this rapidly changing, unforeseen and challenging environment. The challenges are so varied that despite updates in the manual, with all due care, one may come across yet many more instances of ambiguous cases that need to be solved by the examining ballistic expert. The only recourse that then remains is to search for the available literature in books and forensic journals on the subject. It becomes more problematic if there is no apparent solution available in the literature, which could be due to a changed modus operandi or some unknown factor that has not surfaced or been reported earlier. The plausible options in such cases are either to remain non-committal or to modify identification procedures that may need deviation from the norms of the prevailing manual in vogue. Such an expert has to be a research-oriented forensic scientist. As the science of forensic ballistics primarily embraces physical science in dealing with internal, external and terminal ballistics in general, and forensic science in particular, one should preferably have a master's degree in science. Besides educational qualifications, it is also necessary to update the scientific knowledge related to the field of forensic ballistics, from time to time. This necessitates an up-to-date knowledge of a variety of new firearms and ammunition that has entered into the arena of the criminal world. In recent years, the use of illegally produced, substandard unusual firearms that defy known nomenclature and identification criteria has increased exponentially, worldwide, resulting in frequent misleading investigative evidence as has been illustrated above. The expert is required to evaluate the ambiguity and arrive at the right conclusion even by deviating from the normal identification criteria, as the necessity arises. The deviation has to be based on sound scientific principles of forensic ballistics that can stand the acid test of cross-examination and acceptance in the court of law. The experts of today thus must be qualified scientific personnel having appropriate and adequate training and experience in the diverse field of forensic ballistics, to qualify as independent examiners of criminal cases involving firearms.

2.7.1 Adequate training and experience of examining firearm cases

It is well known that human eyes are so remarkably evolved that they can easily differentiate identifying features of one person from another – an undisputed experience of everyday life. But differentiating identifying features of firearms is not so simple. It is an arduous task and needs specialized training and skill. The following gives a brief idea of the basics of firearm identification intricacies.

- Since imperfections of firearms are microscopically small, their static and/or sliding impressions on fired empties and bullets are also minute; they are viewed, examined and compared only under an ocular microscope, usually a comparison microscope. Therefore, it needs very specialized and trained eyes to evaluate minute identifying marks under a comparison microscope for forming an opinion. Although optical microscopic examination is widely used worldwide, ballistic imaging such as IBIS, ALIAS, etc. and the ballistic identification system of digitizing 2D and 3D images for the examination and comparison of fired bullets and cartridge cases have become popular. The BalScan system is very suitable for scanning and comparison of even deformed bullets or bullet fragments and direct scanning of the breech face and firing pin of a firearm. In addition to live examination and comparison, the identification system provides digitizing of bullets/cartridge cases, searching of the database and comparisons.

- In addition to the marks due to random imperfections, one also finds extraneous marks due to uncontrollable factors of mishandling during the manufacturing process, or of the ammunition at various stages (i.e., packing, transportation, arms dealer storage, or at the end-user point) or before and after firing. They need objective evaluation that is elaborately dealt with in Part III.

In order to qualify as a competent ballistics expert, one must be a qualified, research-oriented, scientific person, preferably a master's degree holder in physical sciences. The expert also must have knowledge of firearms and ammunition that are frequently encountered in crime scenes and especially those firearms that are likely to create unusual, misleading and ambiguous marks on their fired ammunition such as substandard firearms manufactured in clandestine factories or improvised and homemade contraptions. The ballistic expert of today, therefore, should also be the master of handling exceptions as well as just managing the norm.

Above all, the expert must have requisite training for the proper presentation of the scientific evidence in the court of law as a ballistic expert. One should acquire the special skill of explaining scientific details in easily understandable, non-technical ways as far as practicable, when confronted in cross-examination or to clarify issues related to the diverse field of forensic ballistics, relevant to the case. The testimony of such a proficient ballistics expert provides due probative value to the report on the scientific findings of physical exhibits as well as scientific evidence during the trial. This will aid the jury and the court to take appropriate decisions. The critical issue prevailing in the present scenario is whether ballistics experts are infallible. This calls for a proficiency test of the experts.

2.8 Proficiency testing and potential rate of error

The expert is often required to state the known potential rate of error in forming an opinion on firearm–ammunition linkage. The most critical issue now becomes how the potential rate of error can be assessed. A detailed statistical study of the proficiency of the experts on the same is the only plausible solution. This calls for identifying essential parameters for the survey of the probable error rate of opinion on firearm–ammunition linkage.

Foremost is identifying the experts who are to take part in the statistical study. In order to have correct assessment, the expert needs to be a qualified scientific person having adequate training and experience to qualify as an independent examiner for forming such an opinion. Obviously, only such an expert is competent to take part in the statistical study of the potential rate of error. This will ensure minimum error on this count.

Having identified the quality of experts for taking part in the statistical study, the significant parameter is to identify the types of exhibits required for examination and the formation of opinion. One of the procedures adopted for the purpose is usually to fire cartridges from a firearm and mark one or two of them as questioned specimens for each examiner and the other three to five as test specimens. However, it cannot be ensured that all such specimens would carry identifiable characteristic features of the firearm for examination and comparison. Some of them may not carry sufficient identifiable marks, leading to inconclusive opinion. Therefore, for a conclusive opinion, the experts should be provided with only fired ammunition that bears identifying features of the firearm both for the questioned and tests specimens. This will minimize errors on this count. But to examine all fired bullets and cartridge cases is an improbable proposition. The alternative is that all wrong or inconclusive opinion must be verified by an independent competent examiner to ascertain whether there was an error on the part of the expert or it was the nature of the questioned and test samples that has resulted in forming such an opinion. This will minimize error in assessing true potential rate of error.

In this context, the relevant extract of the United States Department of Justice statement on the PCAST report for ensuring scientific validity of forensic methods is reproduced below:

> To date, there have been approximately twenty firearms/toolmarks studies primarily focused on sample classification decisions and resulting error rates. These studies used various experimental designs (black-box, closed-set, partially-open, set-to-set), but have all resulted in a false positive error rate ranging from 0% to just over 1.0%. The overall consistency of these findings when considered as a whole, is a good indicator of what the *Daubert* Court described as a method's "potential rate of error." Importantly, this aggregate rate is very low, giving the overall indication that examiners are very accurate and make few source identification errors. Finally, it is worth noting that PCAST opined that an acceptable error rate should be less than 5%. The aggregate false positive error rate in firearms/toolmarks studies to date falls well below that figure.

2.9 Proficiency test of identifying marks of consecutively rifled barrels (subclass marks)

One of the important issues for proficiency tests relates to the evaluation of subclass marks on bullets fired from consecutively rifled barrels. Hamby et al. (2009) have reported their study on consecutively manufactured barrels in the paper titled, "The identification of bullets fired from 10 consecutively rifled 9mm Ruger pistol barrels: a research project involving 507 participants from 20 countries."

The report showed that although one would expect bullets fired from consecutively rifled barrels to display subclass characteristics, this was not an issue for the 502 participants who were properly trained firearm examiners and the test fired bullets were recovered in good condition. The study also showed that statements about the inability of examiners to link fired bullets to consecutively rifled barrels were incorrect. Furthermore, the fact that the unknown bullets were correctly identified and there was no actual error showed that the test procedure to ascribe bullets fired from consecutively rifled barrel is reproducible worldwide.

3

Admissibility of Ballistics Expert Evidence in Criminal Trials in India

In India, ballistics expert evidence is admissible under section 45 of the Evidence Act of 1872 and section 293 of the Code of Criminal Procedure 1973 amended in 2006.

Section 45 of the Evidence Act of 1872 reads as follows:

> OPINIONS OF THIRD PERSONS, WHEN RELEVANT.
>
> 45. When the court has to form an opinion upon a point of foreign law, or of science or art, or as to identity of handwriting [or finger impressions], the opinion on that point of persons especially skilled in such foreign law, science or art [or in questions as to identity of handwriting or finger impressions] are relevant facts. Such persons are called experts.

3.1 Section 45 of the Evidence Act and ballistic expert evidence

Expert opinion in criminal cases of shooting incidents relates to the scientific examination of physical exhibits recovered from the victim's body, crime scene, and from the possession or at the instance of the accused. The subject matter of the opinion relates to the specialized field of science of forensic ballistics and wound ballistics of forensic medicine. Although section 45 of the Evidence Act makes specific mention that an opinion upon a point of science 'is admissible', it does not mention the specific branches of science to which the Act pertains. In this context, the Supreme Court of India in the case *State through CBI, New Delhi v. S J Chaudhary* (1996) has held that the expression "science or art" in Section 45 of Evidence Act 1872 is "of wide import" and that:

> Each of the words "science" and "art" has to be construed widely to include within its ambit the opinion of an expert in each branch of these subjects.

DOI: 10.4324/9781351023863-4

The term "science" in the Act is construed to include the science of forensic ballistics and wound ballistics, and opinion on these subjects is admissible under section 45 of the Evidence Act. The only rider, as per the Act, is that the opinion must be from an especially skilled person in the subject, called an expert. To qualify as an expert, one must have adequate training and experience in the specialized field of expertise and must have made a special study of the subject. This aids the court to decide whether the witness is truly a skilled expert competent to form and testify an opinion on the subject. In view of this, it has now become customary for the expert to place on record their qualifications, training, experience and research in the examination in chief.

It has also been held in the case *State of HP v. Jai Lal* (1999) that "the report submitted by an expert does not go in evidence automatically. He is to be examined as a witness in Court and has to face cross-examination."

3.1.1 Admissibility of medical reports and evidence under section 45 of the Evidence Act

The medico-legal/post-mortem reports and testimony of a medical doctor on firearm injuries or wound ballistics are admissible under section 45 of the Evidence Act. The medical expert must be qualified in the discipline of medical science.

3.2 Section 293 of the Code of Criminal Procedure 1973

Section 293 of the Code of Criminal Procedure 1973 reads as:

> Reports of certain Government scientific experts
>
> (1) Any document purporting to be a report under the hand of a Government scientific expert to whom this section applies, upon any matter or thing duly submitted to him for examination or analysis and report in the course of any proceeding under this Code, may be used as evidence in any inquiry, trial or other proceeding under this Code.
> (2) The Court may, if it thinks fit, summon and examine any such expert as to the subject-matter of his report.
> (3) Where any such expert is summoned by a Court, and he is unable to attend personally, he may, unless the Court has

expressly directed him to appear personally, depute any responsible officer working with him to attend the Court, if such officer is conversant with the facts of the case and can satisfactorily depose in Court on his behalf.

(4) This section applies to the following Government scientific experts, namely:
   (a) any Chemical Examiner or Assistant Chemical Examiner to Government;
   (b) the Chief Inspector of Explosives;
   (c) the Director of the Finger Print Bureau;
   (d) the Director, Haffkeine Institute, Bombay;
   (e) the Director, Deputy Director or Assistant Director of a Central Forensic Science Laboratory or a State Forensic Science Laboratory;
   (f) the Serologist to the Government.

3.2.1 Admissibility of ballistics expert evidence under section 293 of the Code of Criminal Procedure 1973

Pursuant to subsection 4(e) of 293 of the Code of Criminal Procedure 1973, the reports of the Director, Assistant Director (Ballistics) and Deputy Director (Ballistics) of a central forensic science laboratory or a state forensic science laboratory have been made admissible as evidence without their testimony in the court. This remained inapplicable to government experts who were junior in hierarchy such as a senior or a junior scientific officer of a state or central forensic science laboratory, and so also to those who were designated differently, irrespective of their hierarchy (other than Assistant Director and Deputy Director), such as principal scientific officer, scientist, etc.

3.2.2 Amendments to admissibility of ballistics expert evidence under section 293 of the Code of Criminal Procedure 1973

In 2006, amendments to the Code of Criminal Procedure 1973 were enacted, which read as:

In section 293 of the principal Act, in sub section (4),
   (a) for clause (b), the following clause shall be substituted, namely:
   "(b) the Chief Controller of Explosives;";
   (b) after clause (f), the following clause shall be added, namely:-

"(g) any other Government scientific expert specified, by notification, by the Central Government for this purpose."

The amended subsection 4 which enlarged the scope of section 293 by including other government scientific experts may now be read as:

(4) This Section applies to the following Government scientific experts, namely:

(a) any Chemical Examiner or Assistant Chemical Examiner to Government;
(b) the Chief Controller of Explosives;
(c) the Director of the Finger Print Bureau;
(d) the Director, Haffkeine Institute, Bombay;
(e) the Director, Deputy Director or Assistant Director of a Central Forensic Science Laboratory or a State Forensic Science Laboratory;
(f) the Serologist to the Government;
(g) any other Government scientific expert specified by notification by the Central Government for the purpose.

Consequent upon the provisions of section 293(4)(g), other scientists of government institutions engaged in forensic work, besides forensic laboratory scientific experts whose reports were not admissible under section 293(4)(e), have been and are being included by specific government notification as and when deemed necessary.

This amendment has significantly influenced the admissibility of government ballistic expert's reports in criminal trials in India. This provision of exhibiting ballistics experts reports as evidence without their testimony is routinely adopted in almost all present-day criminal trials in India. In such cases, it evidently implies that:

a) Their reports are deemed to be from experts in the field by virtue of the scientific posts they hold in forensic laboratories or other notified government scientific institutes irrespective of their designation and hierarchy.
b) Their reports are deemed to be based on reliable principles of the science of forensic firearm identification and the methodologies they adopt are deemed to be undisputed.
c) Their reports are deemed to be correct and legally admissible as evidence without providing the requisite opportunity to the defending attorney to cross-examine them.

Other significant issues relating to section 293 of the Code of Criminal Procedure worth mentioning are:

- There exists provision under section 293 of the Code of Criminal Procedure to summon any such expert to examine the subject matter of the report, if the court thinks it fit. The court may also summon the expert on the request of prosecution or defence, if it deems fit. This assumes great forensic significance especially if there is no eye witness to the shooting incident. The ballistic evidence of linkage of fired bullets and empties with the accused weapon acts as very strong circumstantial evidence to connect the crime with the criminal through the weapon of offence. This is also so if the eye witnesses is either unreliable or neither reliable nor unreliable. The fact is, even in such cases, this provision often remains unused.
- The testimony of private ballistic experts does not come under the purview of section 293 of the Code of Criminal Procedure and remains admissible under section 45 of the Evidence Act. Private ballistics experts often represent the defence attorney to provide expert opinion on case-related issues including that of the evidence of the government expert. Their usual role, however, is that of a consultant to help the representing defence attorney to prepare a questionnaire for cross-examination of the government ballistic expert and assist the attorney in the court during the expert's testimony, if needed. They are also allowed to cross-examine the government expert if the court deems it fit.
- The evidence law of section 293 of the Code of Criminal Procedure is not applicable to medical doctors. The medical expert evidence on wound ballistics remains admissible under section 45 of the Evidence Act.

Key note: *The nomenclature of the Indian Penal Code (IPC) and of the Criminal Procedure Court (CRPC) have recently been changed. The evidence law, and the law for admissibility of reports for experts, as and when amended, need to be updated accordingly.*

PART II

INVESTIGATIVE ASPECTS IN CRIMINAL TRIALS INVOLVING FIREARMS

4

Introduction to the Investigation of Gunfire Crime and the Basics of Firearms and Ammunition

The investigation of criminal incidents of gunfire plays a vital role in the dissemination of justice. The enforcement agency takes up the investigation of the crime, immediately after it is reported by the victim or an eyewitness or informer. It begins with the preliminary investigation of the eyewitness who reports the criminal incident. The eyewitness gives a graphic picture of the criminal incident. It usually centres around firing at the victim that caused grievous injuries or death. It forms the basis of filing of the first information report (FIR) and initiation of the investigation against the suspect/accused. The witness invariably provides a strong investigative lead about the accused/suspect.

Once the suspect is apprehended, the story of the criminal incident usually changes.

i. Either the allegation of firing at the victim is outright rejected
ii. Or an alternative circumstance that led to the alleged firing is admitted with an undue emphasis on having no criminal intent to fire at the victim and that it was not an act of felony. Some of the circumstances of admitted firing, which are often put forward by the suspect or the defence in a criminal trial, are as follows:
   - That it was an accidental fire:
     a) due to mishandling of the firearm by an unwary person
     b) due to struggle between the assailant and the victim
     c) due to a firearm that was prone to accidental discharge.

DOI: 10.4324/9781351023863-6

- That it was a fire in self-defence
  - a) to protect the life of self and/or family
  - b) to discharge official duties.
- That it was a fire in the air
  - a) to celebrate an occasion
  - b) to disburse a protesting crowd
  - c) to scare an attacking person/parties/crowd.
- That it was a cross firing between rival parties.
- That it was an act of road rage resulting in fire.
- That it was a fire under the influence of drugs or alcohol.
- That it was an act of suicide and not of murder.

One often comes across such conflicting assertions, even though both victim (or eyewitness) and the assailant are true witnesses to the crime. It becomes essential for the investigator to look for evidence other than ocular evidence to unveil the truth. The only recourse, under the circumstances, is to look for physical evidence that may provide necessary inference to corroborate or reject the assertions of either. This calls for a thorough understanding of the issues related to the investigative aspect of physical clues. To do so, a thorough knowledge of the following must be known to the investigators.

- What constitutes physical evidence in criminal cases involving firearms?
- Which physical clue needs scientific examination to corroborate and prove or disprove the hypothesis put forward by either party?
- What investigative steps would ensure an effective search and seizure of physical clues for each type of firearms that are commonly met in crime?

The most important physical evidence in criminal trials relates to the weapon of offence or defence, which in case of gunfire crime is obviously the firearm used in the crime and the ammunition it fired. This entails, foremost, the necessity of having familiarity with the firearm and ammunition that are frequently used in crime and their forensic significance. This does not necessarily mean that the investigator needs to be a firearm expert; it is neither feasible nor desirable. What is required is a meaningful understanding of the makeup of firearms and ammunition and their forensic significance with special reference to various types of firearms that are commonly used in crime. It is not only important for investigators, but equally important for attorneys as well, as well as professionals and personnel associated directly or indirectly with the criminal trial involving firearms. It will help the investigator to achieve an effective zero-error investigation and will also equip the defence with a ready reckoner for a fruitful cross-examination.

4.1 Basic understanding of the general makeup of a firearm and ammunition

4.1.1 General makeup of a firearm

A firearm has essentially three parts. They are the barrel, the body or action and a hand grip or a stock and butt.

4.1.1.1 Barrel

The barrel is the most important part of the firearm. It is a hollow cylinder made of alloy steel of high tensile strength and elasticity.

A brief description of functional parts of the barrel:

The *rear end of the barrel* is known as the breech and the front end is known as the muzzle. The provision of a chamber for housing a cartridge is made at the rear end of the barrel. On firing, the projectile contained in the cartridge is propelled by the gaseous discharge of the propellant.

The *interior of the barrel* through which the gaseous discharge and projectile travels is known as the bore. The bore may be grooved or non-grooved. A number of parallel spiral grooves are cut longitudinally with a twist inside the bore of a grooved barrel. A grooved bore is known as a rifled bore. The raised portions between the grooves are known as lands, and firearms having grooves and lands are known as rifled firearms. They are designated by their bore dimensions. The bore dimension, though nominal, is specific. It is the shortest distance between the opposite lands, measured in inches or in millimetres such as .38", .32", 9 mm, 5.65 mm, 7.92 mm, etc. The bore dimension of rifled firearms is known as the calibre of the rifled firearm. The majority of firearms encountered worldwide in crime are rifled firearms, such as pistols, revolvers, carbines, rifles, etc.

A non-grooved bore is known as a smooth bore, and a non-grooved firearm as a smooth-bore firearm. Firearms that fall into this category, which are frequently encountered in crimes, are shotguns. Their bore diameter is larger than rifled firearms. They are measured and designated differently than rifled firearms. Their bore diameter is indirectly assessed/measured as equivalent to the diameter of a spherical lead shot that exactly fits the smooth-bore firearm. The number of such spherical shots that weigh one pound is designated as the bore of the firearm. If the spherical lead shot that fits the smooth-bore firearm weighs 1/12th of a pound, then the firearm is designated as a 12-gauge firearm or simply a 12-bore firearm. If the spherical lead shot that fits the smooth-bore firearm weighs 1/16th of a pound, it is a 16-bore firearm. The same is applicable for a 20-bore or 28-bore firearm. Traditional shotguns are smooth-bore firearms and are designated as 12-bore shotguns, 16-bore shotguns, etc.

There are exceptions in designating rifled and smooth-bore firearms. Lager bore dimension firearms, whether grooved or not, are designated by gauge or bore and smaller bore dimension firearms by inches or millimetres. The traditional .410″ musket is a smooth-bore firearm whose bore dimension is less than 32-bore. Similarly rifled firearms whose bore dimensions are more than .60″ are designated as 10-bore, 8-bore, etc.

The designated bore/or calibre of the firearm, the make of the firearm and the serial number of the firearm are invariably marked on the firearm. This information helps to establish the owner, especially if it is a licensed firearm.

4.1.1.2 Body or action mechanism

The barrel is attached to the body, which houses the action mechanism of the firearm. The action mechanism can easily be understood by knowing the sequence of firing operations.

Loading and locking

To begin with, a live cartridge is loaded in the chamber. Thereafter, the barrel is locked firmly with the body. The part of the body against which the base of the loaded cartridge is firmly seated at the rear is known as the breech block of the firearm. A secured locking mechanism in the body ensures that the barrel does not open during the travel of the projectile inside the bore and there is no rearward escape of gases. This makes the firearm safe during the travel of the projectile inside the bore on firing.

Cocking and firing

Cocking and firing operations are usually achieved by the hammer and trigger, actuated by a spring. A rearward movement of the hammer compresses the main spring, and the trigger is engaged in the rear position. This position is known as the cocked position. To initiate firing of the cartridge, the provision of a firing pin is made in the body. The firing pin is invariably either an integral part of a hammer or is spring driven with or without a hammer. On pressing the trigger, the sear, which connects the trigger with the initiation of the firing mechanism, is disengaged resulting in falling of the hammer and initiating the firing processes.

Propelling of the projectile and gaseous discharge residues

The firing pin, whether integral or spring driven, hits the primer of the loaded cartridge. This results in the crushing of the priming mixture, thereby producing flame. The flame is communicated to the propellant charge through flash holes. This ignites the propellant inside the cartridge. The ignited propellant rapidly converts into gases and develops a very high temperature and pressure. This results in expansion of the cartridge case inside the chamber. The cartridge case touches the interior of the barrel and seals the backward escape of gases. The forward-moving gases unseat the projectile from the cartridge and moves forward inside the bore until it is projected out of the muzzle with a high velocity along with the gaseous discharge. Being very light, the gaseous discharge travels only a very short distance. The distance may vary between a few inches to a couple of feet depending on the type of firearm. If hot, the emerging gases burn or char the skin and singe the hair. The forward-moving hot gases are cooled very quickly due to their rapid dissipation in the atmosphere and produce a blackening effect on the clothing or on bare skin of human targets. The emerging gaseous discharge following the projectile also carries unburned or partially burned propellant particles. These particles, being heavier than gaseous particles, move farther and are embedded in the skin, giving the appearance of a tattooing effect, known as powder tattooing.

The presence of charring, blackening and powder particles/powder tattooing on the clothing or on the bare skin of human targets, mentioned in the medico-legal/post-mortem report, provides valuable physical evidence of a close-range firing that may prove helpful to corroborate the hypothesis of suicide, struggle, accidental fire, self-defence, etc.

Extraction and ejection

After the projectile and gaseous discharge residues are propelled out of the barrel, it becomes necessary to remove the fired empty. The fired empty is first extracted from the chamber and thereafter ejected out of the firearm. For this purpose, provision of an extractor and an ejector is made in the firearm. The empty is unloaded either by removing it manually or by the extractor and the ejector of the firearm. This empties the chamber to make room to load and fire a fresh round.

All the sequential firing operations can be carried out either manually or by the gaseous discharge produced on firing a cartridge.

4.1.1.3 Hand grip or a stock and butt – handguns and shoulder firearms

A handgrip or a stock is attached to the body for a firm hold while aiming and firing the firearm. A handgrip is provided to hold a short-barrelled firearm and a stock to a long-barrelled firearm. Short-barrelled firearms are known as handguns as they can conveniently be aimed and fired by one hand. Revolvers and pistols are short-barrelled handguns, and they have handgrips.

On the other hand, for a firm hold of a long-barrelled firearm, one needs a shoulder support while aiming and firing. A stock and butt are attached to the body to provide the necessary shoulder support to a long-barrelled firearm. Long-barrelled firearms that need a shoulder support are known as shoulder firearms. Rifles and shotguns are long-barrelled shoulder firearms, and they are provided with a stock and butt.

4.1.2 General makeup of a cartridge

A cartridge is a complete ammunition which essentially comprises of:

- a cartridge case
- primer
- propellant

- wadding, if any
- projectile/s.

Each component has a specific purpose. The cartridge case houses all the other components of the cartridge. The primer contains a priming composition that initiates the firing operation. The propellant, a low explosive, generates gases and develops a very high temperature and pressure inside the barrel that propels the projectile with a high velocity at considerable distance, which can cause grievous injury or death to human targets. The wadding, if any, is like a seal that acts as a barrier to prevent gases from escaping from behind and is propelled out along with the projectile. The essential components of the cartridge that are left behind after firing are the fired empty, fired projectile including fired wads, if any, and dissipated discharge residue deposits.

After gaining familiarity with the general makeup of firearm and cartridge components, it is necessary to become acquainted with their evidentiary values and possible investigative leads.

A firearm is seldom recovered or found at the crime scene. The assailant does not part with the firearm after firing at the victim, unless apprehended while committing the crime. Usually, therefore, the only available physical evidence is the components of the fired ammunition such as fired empties, fired projectiles, and discharge deposits of primer and propellants. One needs to know first the evidentiary values of fired ammunition and the possible investigative leads they provide, especially for the search and seizure of the suspected firearm.

5

Evidentiary values of fired ammunition in criminal trials and investigative leads

5.1 Evidentiary values of fired empty in criminal trials and investigative leads

It is the physical evidence of a fired empty that helps in establishing the perpetrator of a crime through the weapon of offence. It provides investigative leads to broadly identify the type of firearm that was used for committing the crime and its recovery for establishing linkage of the empty with the suspected firearm.

5.1.1 Investigative leads to broadly identify the type of firearm from fired empty

Foremost to ascertain is the calibre/bore of the firearm that fired the empty. This is usually possible by examining the base of the cartridge as the calibre/bore is normally marked on the base of the cartridge. Having ascertained the calibre or bore, it is necessary to look for investigative leads to broadly identify the type of firearm. Differentiation of the type of firearm can be invariably and easily made from examination of the fired empty. The significant types are mentioned below.

5.1.1.1 Rifled or smooth-bore shotguns

It is the construction material of the cartridge case that differentiates between rifled and smooth-bore shotguns. Whereas the cartridge cases of rifled firearms are made of copper alloy, usually brass, the materials used for cartridge cases of smooth-bore firearms are mostly plastics, although a special type of traditional paper continues to be used, too.

 DOI: 10.4324/9781351023863-7

5.1.1.2 Low- or high-velocity firearm

Firearms that develop subsonic velocity are usually known as low-velocity firearms. Pistols, revolvers and shotguns are usually low-velocity firearms. Firearms that develop supersonic velocity are known as high-velocity firearms. Hunting rifles and service and assault rifles are high-velocity firearms.

It is the shape of the cartridge at the mouth which differentiates between these two. Cartridges that have parallel walls from base to mouth are used for low-velocity firearms, while those with a bottle-necked shape at the mouth are used for high-velocity firearms.

For high-power cartridges, the space required for a heavy-load propellant is far greater, compared to that of low-power cartridges. The construction features of the cartridge are therefore modified accordingly. To accommodate a heavy load of propellant, the provision of extra space is created by making the mouth bottle-necked. The bottle-necked features of the cartridge provide the necessary investigative lead that the firearm used was a high-powered firearm.

5.1.1.3 Manually loaded or auto loader (semi-/fully automatic) firearms

It is the shape of the base of the cartridge which differentiates between manually loaded and auto loader firearms. While the base of cartridges for a manual-loading firearm has a rim, it is rimless for semiautomatic/automatic firearms, which have a magazine for loading and firing number of rounds. A rimmed cartridge has a flange at the base; instead of the flange, the base of a rimless cartridge is grooved.

Field examination of the constructional material, shape of the mouth and shape of the base of the fired empty, coupled with examination of base markings for the calibre/bore, provides necessary investigative leads that may help in the recovery of the suspected firearm. Once the suspected firearm is recovered, it is usually possible for a forensic firearms expert to establish the firearm–empty linkage by scientific examination of the fired empty and the suspect firearm.

After recovery of the fired cartridge case (the empty) and the suspect firearm, it is mandatory for the investigator to seek expert opinion as to whether the seized empty had been fired from the suspect firearm. A positive opinion would evidently connect the crime with the criminal weapon and therefore with the owner, especially if the firearm is a licensed one. A negative opinion, on the other hand, eliminates the suspected firearm.

5.1.2 Negative opinion and acquittal

A negative opinion – that the fired empty had not been fired from the suspected firearm – may ordinarily lead to acquittal especially if the eyewitness is untrustworthy. While restoring the judgment of acquittal passed by the trial court by relying on an expert's negative opinion, the Supreme Court of India in the case *Joginder Singh v. State of Haryana* (2013) held:

> [T]he learned trial Judge, relying on the ballistic report, Ext. P.UU, opined that the .12 bore fired cartridges cases C1 to C4 were fired from a fire-arm but not from DBBB gun W/1, Ext 15, the weapon that was seized from the custody of the accused Joginder Singh. He also took note of the fact that the ballistic report though referred to the mutilated pellets that had hit the deceased yet did not give any opinion. These findings were recorded to form an opinion [...] that the prosecution had failed to establish its case beyond reasonable doubt against the main accused Joginder Singh and resultantly against the other accused persons also and, accordingly, acquitted all of them [...] In view of the aforesaid analysis [...] the judgment passed by the High Court is set aside and that of the learned trial judge is restored.

5.2 Continuity of the chain of evidence – recovery of fired empty, whether genuine or doubtful?

Continuity of the chain of evidence is a critical aspect of criminal trials involving firearms. It needs to be established that the seized physical exhibits are indeed the ones that have been recovered from the crime scene or from the possession or at the instance of the accused. The onus lies on the investigator to establish the continuity of the chain of evidence, especially if the seized physical exhibit is the fired cartridge case/empty, because its linkage with the firearm connects the crime with the weapon and consequently with its owner or possessor as the perpetrator of the crime. The defence, especially in India, very often challenges the recovery of a fired empty as doubtful and, if it is proved so, the expert's opinion on the same becomes redundant. It has no legal validity. The court accepts or rejects the defence plea depending upon the investigative procedures that have been followed during the investigation of the case, whether they are as per requisite norms or there are lapses. Some of the significant court rulings on such issues are worth mentioning.

5.2.1 Not sealed at the time of seizure and inordinate delay

While discussing the inordinate delay in forwarding the seized cartridge case, the Supreme Court of India in case state of *Ghudan v. State of Madhya Pradesh* (2003) held:

> We are also in agreement with the finding of the High Court that it is not safe to place reliance on the report of the ballistic expert because it is an admitted fact that the empties which were sent to the ballistic expert after six months were not sealed at the time of seizure. Therefore, the identity of the empties seized from the place of incident and those tested by the expert cannot be safely tallied.

It is mandatory for investigators to seal the seized physical exhibits, especially the fired empty, in the presence of witness, duly signed to make the seizure genuine and thus ensure continuity of the chain of evidence.

5.2.2 Empty and firearm seized on two different dates but sent together

The evidential value of expert opinion on the linkage of the fired empty with the seized firearm forms strong scientific corroborating evidence to link the criminal through the weapon. It is especially so if the suspect firearm is seized from the possession of the suspect after the empty has been seized from the place of occurrence of that crime and that, too, on two different dates. Its utility in the decision of the criminal case depends upon the investigator's approach in forwarding the same to the forensic expert for examination and report.

While discussing the evidential value of the forensic report on the linkage of an empty with the suspect firearm in a murder case, *Nirmal Singh v. State of Punjab* (1983), the High Court held:

> It is stated by A.S.I. Kanikkar Singh that he found an empty cartridge at the place of occurrence which he sent to the Forensic Science Laboratory along with the gun (Exhibit P/28) recovered from Nirmal Singh, accused. Dr. S. N Sharma, Assistant Director, Forensic Science Laboratory (PW16), ... that the test conducted in the laboratory showed that the said cartridge had been fired from the gun Exhibit P/28. Much reliance

> has been placed by the prosecution on this evidence and it is contended that the empty cartridge recovered from the place of occurrence having been connected with the gun found in possession of Nirmal Singh would prove the complicity of Nirmal Singh in the crime. This argument would have had great force if the crime cartridge had been sent to the laboratory before the recovery of the gun from Nirmal Singh. It is, however, admitted that the cartridge as well as the gun were sent to the laboratory by the Police on 27.6.1982 i.e. one month after the occurrence. As such a possibility cannot be excluded that the so-called crime cartridge had been fired from gun Exhibit P/28 after it was recovered from Nirmal Singh and then the cartridge and the gun were sent to the laboratory for testing. No special value can, therefore, be attached to the report of Dr. Sharma.

5.2.3 Firearm and empty recovered but not sent for expert opinion – a serious investigative lapse

Keeping in view the importance of an expert's opinion, it must be borne in mind that an investigative lapse in forwarding the seized empties and firearm may reflect adversely not only on the decision of the case but also on the creditworthiness of the prosecution/investigator. While discussing a prosecution lapse in seeking expert opinion, the Supreme Court of India in the case *State of Punjab v. Sukhwant Singh* (1995) held:

> There is yet another infirmity in this case. We find that whereas an empty had been recovered by PW6, ASI Raghubir Singh from the spot and a pistol along with some cartridges were seized from the possession of the appellant at the time of his arrest, yet the prosecution, for reasons best known to it, did not send the recovered empty and the seized pistol to the ballistic expert for the examination and expert opinion. Comparison could have provided link evidence between the crime and the accused. This again is an omission on the part of the prosecution for which no explanation has been furnished either in the trial court or before us. It hardly needs to be emphasised that in cases where injuries are caused by firearms, the opinion of the Ballistic Expert is of a considerable importance where both the firearm and the crime cartridge are recovered during the investigation to connect an accused with the crime. *Failure to produce the expert opinion before the trial court in such cases affects the creditworthiness of the prosecution case to a great extent.*

5.3 Whether the investigator's lapse must lead to acquittal – some guiding principles

In this context, the Supreme Court of India, in the case *State of Karnataka v. K. Yarappa Reddy* (1999), held:

> It can be a guiding principle that as investigation is not the solitary area for judicial scrutiny in a criminal trial, the conclusion of the court in the case cannot be allowed to depend solely on the probity of investigation. It is well settled that even if the investigation is illegal or even suspicious the rest of the evidence must be scrutinized independently of the impact of it. Otherwise, the criminal trial will plummet to the level of the investigating officers ruling the roost. The court must have predominance and pre-eminence in criminal trials over the action taken by investigating officers. Criminal justice should not be made a casualty for the wrongs committed by the investigating officers in the case. In other words, if the court is convinced that the testimony of a witness to the occurrence is true the court is free to act on it albeit the investigating officer's suspicious role in the case.

A similar view has been held by the Supreme Court in the case *Hema v. State of Tamilnadu* (2013):

> It is clear that merely because of some defect in the investigation, lapse on the part of the investigating officer, it cannot be a ground for acquittal. Further, even if there had been negligence on the part of the investigating agency or omissions, etc., it is the obligation on the part of the court to scrutinise the prosecution evidence, abhors such lapses, to find out whether the said evidence is reliable or not and whether such lapses affect the object of finding out the truth.

6

Fired projectiles as evidentiary clues in criminal trials and investigative leads

The fired projectile is another important form of physical evidence that helps in establishing the perpetrator of a crime through the weapon of offence. Projectiles are almost always recovered, either from the victim's body or from the place of the criminal incident. A fired projectile carries greater evidential value than a fired cartridge because it is the projectile which causes injuries. The investigative leads that a projectile can provide, especially for the search for a suspected firearm, must be known to the investigators.

Foremost is the general shape of the projectile which differentiates between rifled and smooth-bore firearms. Whereas a single conical projectile (known as a bullet) is used to fire from a rifled firearm, a large number of spherical lead alloy shots (also known as pellets) are used to fire from smooth-bore firearms such as shotguns.

The evidentiary values of bullets are different from those of spherical shots, and they are discussed separately.

6.1 Bullets as evidentiary clues in criminal trials and investigative leads

Bullets are essentially meant to be fired from a rifled barrel that has grooves and raised lands. The evidentiary value of fired bullets, therefore, depends upon the marks they imprint due to the lands and grooves. During their travel inside the grooved barrel, they imprint the exact number of lands and grooves it has, their width (whether equal or different), the angle/slant of lands/grooves (whether towards the right or left, known as right- and left-handed rifling) and finally the pitch of rifling. These parameters represent the rifling specifications

DOI: 10.4324/9781351023863-8

which are specific for a particular make, model and calibre of rifled firearm, and are known as class characteristic rifling marks. Even one parameter is enough for the differentiation and elimination of improbable firearm. A fired bullet having six lands and grooves eliminates firearms having five or seven lands and grooves. The inclination of lands and grooves towards the left for a left-handed rifling eliminates rifled firearms having right-handed rifling, and the same applies to differences in land or groove widths. Class characteristic parameters on fired bullets prove helpful in identifying the probable suspect firearms and eliminating the improbable. Figures 6.1a and 6.1b illustrate class characteristic rifling marks on fired bullets.

A regularly updated databank of rifling specifications enables the forensic firearm expert to ascertain the probable make and model of the firearm from the fired bullet.

The investigator must seek an expert opinion to ascertain the make and model of the firearm that fired the evidence bullet recovered from the victim's body or from the crime scene. Once the opinion of an expert on calibre, make and model of the suspected rifled firearm is known to the investigator, it becomes easier to search for the suspected firearm – primarily because the calibre, make and model of the rifled firearms are invariably mentioned on the firearm.

Figure 6.1a Right-handed rifling marks on fired bullets

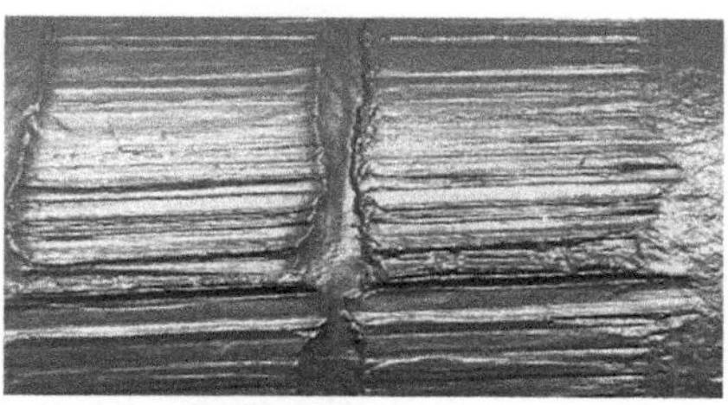

Figure 6.1b Left-handed rifling marks on fired bullets

6.1.1 Recovery of suspected rifled firearm and seized evidence bullet

Once the probable firearm carrying class characteristic parameters similar to that of the evidence bullet is seized, it is possible for the expert to establish whether the said evidence bullet had been fired from the suspected rifled firearm. This is a laboratory expert's routine scientific examination. The expert forms an opinion by comparing the striations present on the evidence bullet which represent the identifying features of the rifled barrel with those on the test bullets fired from the suspected rifled firearm.

After recovery of the fired bullet and the suspected rifled firearm, it is mandatory for the investigator to forward and seek expert opinion as to whether the evidence bullet recovered from the victim or from the crime scene had been fired from the suspected firearm. A positive opinion would connect the crime with the criminal weapon and therefore with the owner, especially if the bullet is recovered from the victim's body and the firearm is a licensed one. This assumes great forensic significance if there is no eyewitness.

6.2 Spherical shots or pellets as evidentiary clues in criminal trials and investigative leads

Cartridges fired from smooth-bore firearms are generally loaded with a large number of spherical shots/pellets of lead alloy of varying sizes. The size of the shot/pellet does not provide investigative leads to ascertaining the bore of the shotgun unless it is a single ball. It is mainly because the same-sized shots/pellets are loaded in shotgun cartridges irrespective of the bore of the shotgun. Only the number of shots/pellets changes. The investigative leads that they provide are very limited. The size differentiates its usage, whether it is for hunting big game or shooting small game. They are designated differently for bigger and smaller shots, and they differ from one country to the other. The investigator needs to be familiar with their designation.

- Big game hunting shots and their designation

  The bigger shots are popularly known as buckshot in the US (American standards). They are used for big game hunting and their sizes vary with the type of the game. They are designated as Buckshot (000), Buckshot (00), etc. The bigger shots for large game are known as LG shots in British/Indian specifications. They are SG for small game, SSG and so on. Their size and weight vary accordingly and so also the number of shots loaded.

- Small game shots and their designation

  Smaller-sized shots are usually known as pellets. They are designated differently by shot number which represents the number of shots loaded in the cartridge such as No.1, No.4, No.6, No.10, etc. Their size may vary with the country and the number of pellets that weigh one ounce/28.3 grams, which is the usual unit of load in cartridges having shots/pellets. The British/Indian specifications cartridges have 100 pellets in No.1, 270 pellets in No. 6, 600 in No.10 and so on. The size of the spherical shot /pellet may be as low as .050″ for Number 12 and as high as .38″ for Buckshot (0000). The normal load of a 12-bore 2½″/65mm shotgun cartridge is usually 30 grams.

6.2.1 Dispersion of shots/pellets as evidentiary clues and investigative leads

The dispersion of pellets in shotgun fire provides investigative leads to assess the distance of fire, which helps in the reconstruction of the crime scene. When a shotgun cartridge having multiple pellets is fired, the pellets start spreading as soon as they leave the barrel. The area of dispersion of pellets increases with the increasing distance of fire. Experiments have shown that the dispersion increases roughly in a conical shape and there exists a rough correlation between the distance of fire and the area of spread of pellets – i.e. the area of dispersion of pellets in inches roughly corresponds to the distance of fire in yards.

This correlation, though rough, serves as a valuable guide in the field investigation. This is an important investigative lead for assessing the probable distance from which the assailant had fired at the victim. A 4-inch dispersion is expected from a firing distance of about 4 yards, 10-inch dispersion from 10 yards, 30-inch from 30 yards and so on. Although it looks quite simple to assess the firing distance, it is certainly not so. Let us take a simple example of a 50-inch dispersion of pellets striking a small-sized target of 20 inches. Obviously, part of the shots would not hit the target. This would result in the presence of only a part of the total dispersion, which may be a maximum of 20 inches in this case. This would correspond to a firing distance of 20 yards instead of the actual firing distance of 50 yards corresponding to 50-inch dispersion. Any assessment alone on the part of the total dispersion would be wrong. This signifies that the size of the target is an important rider. It must be taken into consideration while assessing the firing distance on targets whether human or an object such as wooden door.

It is the human target that is of greatest concern in criminal trials. A human target is a small target and the entire pellet dispersion that can be accommodated is also comparatively smaller. It is necessary to ascertain the maximum distance up to which the entire pellet dispersion can be found on a human target. One may expect a dispersion of 10 to 15 inches as an approximate threshold for a small-sized human target. Experiments carried out by various researchers in the field have proved helpful in the assessment.

When a cartridge is fired from a smooth-bore shotgun, the entire shot charge moves en masse as a single projectile only up to a distance of about 3–4 feet and creates a single big hole of about 1–1½-inch diameter, popularly known as a rat hole. The pellets start separating quickly with the increasing distance and disperse around the central primary hole. They start making separate individual holes surrounding the primary hole from a distance of about 5–6 feet. With the increasing distance, the separation of pellets increases rapidly, and the size of the primary rat hole diminishes. Almost all pellets make individual holes from a range of about 10–12 yards and the primary hole becomes almost non-existent. In the case of buckshot, the individual shots make separate holes from a firing distance of only about 5 yards.

In summary:

i. *A correlation between the spread of pellets in inches and the distance of fire in yards serves as a valuable guide for field investigation, only if the whole pattern is available on the human target.*
ii. *A single big hole of about 1–1½ inches in diameter indicates a close range of fire.*
iii. *Pellet spread, if surrounding the primary central hole, invariably indicates entire pellet pattern available for a rough assessment of firing distance of fire.*

CAUTION

Assessment of the distance of fire from an incomplete shot/pellet pattern alone is virtually only a guess, which is a very risky proposition for field investigation. If one is unable to evaluate whether the dispersion is complete or not, then the safest approach would be to assess the distance of fire only when it is a single rat hole without any scattering of pellets, which is about 3–4 feet.

The above, though it serves as a useful investigative lead, is primarily meant for a rough assessment only during field investigation to corroborate or disprove the statement of the eyewitness or the accused. Investigators are not authorized to form opinion and testify on the same, irrespective of their knowledge, skill and experience. It has no legal validity. It must be understood that opinion on distance of fire is exclusively the domain of forensic firearm and medico-legal experts. Only they are competent to form opinion and testify. The investigator must seek expert opinion for the assessment of approximate distance of fire if it is required to be placed on record.

6.2.1.1 Barrel marks on fired shots/pellets and shotgun cupped cartridge

A forensic firearm expert conducts experimental firings with the suspected firearm in each case, preferably with the same type of ammunition as used in the crime. A similar pellet spread pattern is obtained by firing at various ranges to form opinion on the probable range of fire. It is usually difficult to form opinion beyond a range of 10 yards by comparing the spread of pellets experimentally.

Spherical lead shots/pellets that are placed at the periphery of the cartridge touch the walls of the barrel during their travel inside the bore. They make sliding contacts from the breech to the muzzle end and create striations. Noticeable striations are likely to be imprinted on the peripheral shots/pellets. This results in deformation of peripheral shots/pellets. These are known as stray pellets/flyers. They lose their spherical shape and move farther away from the entire shot charge compared to the others. This makes the spread of pellets wider. The more flyers there are, the wider the pellet spread pattern will be. To minimize the wider spread pattern due to flyers/stray pellets, the provision of a cup is made which accommodates the shots/pellets that are to be loaded in the cartridge. It is the cup and not the peripheral shots which comes in direct contact with the sides of the barrel.

6.3 Wads as evidentiary clues in criminal trials and investigative leads

Wads are an essential component of shotgun cartridges that load a number of spherical shots/pellets. Various construction materials are used for wads, which differentiates the make of the branded cartridge from one to another. They provide valuable clues and investigative leads. To evaluate, investigators are required to be familiar with the variety of wads that are usually loaded in shotgun cartridges and their forensic significance.

6.3.1 Construction material and number of wads

The main purpose of the wad is to provide a barrier to prevent the escape of propellant gases into the shot charge. This is achieved by providing a wad that expands on the expansion of powder gases and seals the bore. For this purpose, a thick cardboard wad having a hole on both sides at the centre, popularly known as an air cushion wad, is provided in traditional shotgun cartridges. In addition to sealing of the bore, it also provides a cushioning effect for the smooth propulsion of shot charge inside the barrel. To protect the air cushion wad from the propellant and the shot charge, the provision of thin cardboard wads, one over the propellant and the other under the shot charge, is made – these are known as over-powder and undershot wads. To close the open mouth, the front end of the cartridge is usually crimped. Alternatively, the provision of an additional thin cardboard wad is made for closing the mouth, known as a closing disc, top wad, or overshot wad. Besides air cushion wads, felt and fibre wads are also used to provide the necessary sealing and cushioning effect. Wads tend to scatter the shot charge cluster, whether travelling ahead or behind. The scattering of pellets increases with the number of wads, thereby affecting the spread of pellet pattern – an inherent drawback of multiple wads in shotgun cartridges.

The modern trend is to minimize the number of wads. The most commonly used configuration is having only one specially designed plastic wad with a crimped mouth which serves all the requisite purposes. Besides constructional material, wads of branded shotgun cartridges also vary in their design, weight and size. They provide significant investigative leads.

6.3.2 Make-up of wads and investigative leads to locate the position of assailant

All the wads contained in a cartridge are propelled out of the muzzle along with the shot charge. Their distance of travel varies with their weight and their position of loading, whether in front or behind the shots. The top wad/closing disc in front of the shot charge, being the lightest, travels the least, and the cushioning/sealing wad, being the heaviest, travels the farthest. Additional wads behind the shots, if any, such as over-powder or undershot wads, would travel to a distance in between the top wad and the sealing wad.

The recovery of wads at the crime scene provides valuable clue about the distance from which the assailant had fired at the victim. If the top wad is recovered, then the position of the firer is the distance up to which top wad travels. If it can travel up to about 6–8 feet, then the position of the firer is also about 6–8 feet to the rear of the place from which it is recovered at the crime scene.

Likewise, the position of the firer can be assessed from the locations of other wads by knowing the approximate maximum distance they can travel.

Although cushioning/sealing wads, such as air cushion, fibre, felt, or plastic wads, travel the farthest, their distance of projection varies widely with the variation in their construction material, shape, size and weight of one make to the other. Therefore, to assess the probable distance, an authenticated experimental result is needed.

In a criminal case of admitted firing, an air cushion wad was found at the place of occurrence. The dispute was over the distance of fire. The prosecution quoted the famous forensic ballistic book by Burrard (1951) and alleged that firing could be possible only from a distance of about 40 feet. But the defence plea was that the distance was far more and not less than 100–120 feet. The fired empty seized in the case was a 12-bore empty of an Indian ordnance factory manufactured cartridge. After exhaustive experiments with the same make, the author opined that air cushion wads loaded in Indian ordnance factory cartridges may travel up to a distance of about 150 feet. Evidently, the experimental results of 40 feet mentioned in the book relate to the firing of cartridges loaded with a lighter-weight air cushion wad compared to that of Indian ordnance factory cartridges.

It is usually not possible to assess, even a very rough estimate, the distance of projection of any of the aforementioned cushioning/sealing wads for the reconstruction of crime scene, unless an authenticated experimental result is in hand. It is the expert who can opine on approximate distance of the cushioning/sealing wad by performing experiments with cartridges having a similar make-up – material, shape, size and weight. This is equally true for other wads.

As the likely distance of travel of each type of wad is different from one to another and from one make to another, not only is the investigator required to ascertain the location of each, but it is equally important to correctly identify the wad's type at each location. This is usually not possible. To avoid incorrect identification:

> *The investigator must make separate sealed parcel for each of the recovered wads found at the crime scene and note their respective distances with respect to the victim or any other reference. This information would help the expert to correctly opine on probable distance of fire for each, which would enable the investigator to assess the probable location of the firer for the reconstruction of the crime scene at its end.*

> **Key note:** *The investigator should neither mix all the recovered wads nor send them mixed in one sealed packet.*

6.3.3 Wads inside the wound and investigative leads for doubtful recovery of fired empty

In a murder case, the wad recovered from the victim's body was a felt wad, but the fired empty that was alleged to have been recovered from the crime scene was a 12-bore Indian ordnance factory manufactured shotgun cartridge which loads cardboard air cushion wads and not felt wads. This led to the obvious conclusion of the doubtful recovery of the fired empty even though it was positively linked with the suspected SBBL gun.

The construction material and make-up of the wad may provide a helpful determining factor for proving doubtful recovery of fired empty. The investigator needs to be cautious on this count because it may adversely affect the worthiness of the investigation.

6.3.4 *Wads inside the wound and investigative leads for distance of fire*

A wad is often found inside the wound. It is extracted by the medical officer who examines the victim and submits medico-legal/post-mortem reports. The examination report essentially mentions the recovery of wads inside the wound, but it usually does not specify whether the recovered wads are sealing/cushioning plastic, felt/fibre wads and/or any other wads that are often loaded in shotgun cartridges. As the distance of travel of different wads varies with their construction material, shape and size, a simple mention that a wad or wad/s have been recovered from the wound may not prove helpful in making an assessment of the probable distance of fire. However, there is always specific mention of the dimension of the wound which lodges the wads. This suggests that it would be helpful to couple the recovery of wads with the specific dimension of the wound for assessing the probable distance of fire from the medico-legal/post-mortem report available to the investigator. The safest distance of fire that can conveniently be assessed is a close range of fire from a distance of about 6 feet or so. In such a case, besides a wound dimension of about 1½-inch diameter, the recovery of wads inside the wound would also be specifically mentioned in the medico-legal/post-mortem report. It is well known and was discussed earlier that the entire shot charge along with all the wads enters en masse into the body causing a big rat hole about 1½ inches in diameter.

Specific mention of the recovery of wads from a big rat hole of about 1½ inches in diameter in the medico-legal/post-mortem report signifies a close range of fire from a distance of about 6–8 feet. Even the top wad travelling in front, despite being the lightest, forces entry into the wound created by the heavy impact of the fast-moving entire shot column from behind.

In addition to the projectile and wads, discharge residues emanating from the primer and propellants are also projected out of the muzzle with high velocity. They also provide significant investigative leads.

6.4 Primer as evidentiary clues in criminal trials and investigative leads

Primer is a crucial component of a cartridge. It contains a very sensitive explosive mixture which initiates the firing processes. It is the gunshot residue (GSR) deposit of the metallic constituent of the priming composition which proves helpful in identifying the shooter. GSR particles are detected usually by automated instrumental analysis such as SEM coupled with EDX, etc. Swabs and adhesive tapes are commonly adopted for lifting GSR particulates. Sample collection needs to be carried out as per the needs of the examining forensic laboratory, preferably the nearest in the vicinity.

A deteriorated chemical composition of the primer may not initiate the firing process even after the primer is hit by the firing pin. This results in a misfired cartridge.

The other evidential importance of the primer is the marks it carries due to striking of the firing pin. The firing pin hit marks on the fired empty are utilized for cartridge–firearm linkage. Although not very common, one also comes across fired cartridges which are devoid of firing pin marks. Phenomena of such occurrences and their investigative aspects are:

- The firing pin hit may perforate the primer. This is popularly known as perforated caps. This results in the absence of firing pin marks on the primer of the fired empty. Figure 6.2a shows a perforated cap.
- The firing pin hit may even blow the primer out of the cartridge. This is popularly known as the fired empty having a blown cap. A small-sized blown primer is invariably

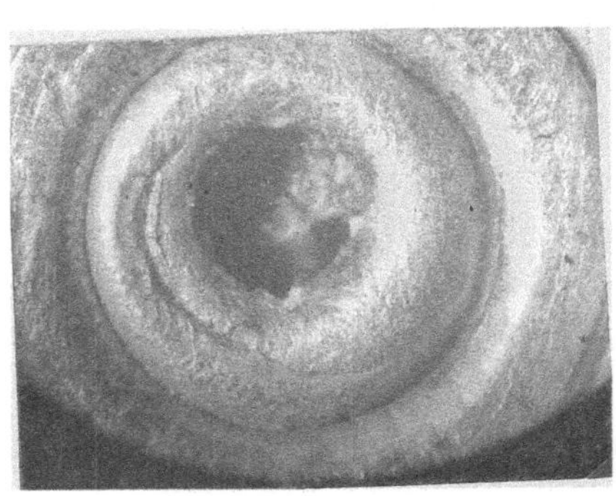

Figure 6.2a A perforated cap

Figure 6.2b A blown cap

impossible to locate and recover. This makes the blown capped fired empty devoid of primer that carried the firing pin marks. Figure 6.2b shows a blown cap.

Although fired empties having perforated and blown caps do not carry firing pin marks, this does not necessarily mean that they are unsuitable for identification. The presence of identifying marks other than firing pin marks cannot be ruled out and expert opinion is a must.

The investigator must forward the seized fired empty for expert opinion, irrespective of perforated or blown caps. It is for the expert to opine whether the said empty can be identified in respect of the questioned firearm.

6.5 Propellants as evidentiary clues and investigative leads

Propellant is the main explosive charge that converts rapidly into gases to propel the projectile. The burning of the total propellant charge loaded in the cartridge is seldom complete. This results in the presence of unburnt and partially burnt propellant particles in the gaseous discharge that are also projected out of the muzzle with considerably high velocity. These may be embedded in the pores of the skin at close range, which appears like tattooing of the skin. This phenomenon is popularly known as powder tattooing. Their distance of projection depends upon the type of the firearm, whether a high- or a low-power firearm. The presence of powder tattooing is generally found well within 3–4 feet in the case of firearms using smokeless powders.

Powder particles are deposited on clothing at close range if the bullet does not hit the victim's bare skin or any other object.

The presence of propellant particles on clothing or powder tattooing on bare skin provides positive proof of close-range fire. The investigator needs to seek expert opinion about the approximate distance of close-range fire that may help in the reconstruction of the crime scene in evaluating criminal cases of suicide, struggle, self-defence or murder.

6.5.1 *Shape and size of propellant for differentiation of low- and high-velocity firearms*

The expanding gases emanating from the burning of propellant unseats the projectile. It moves forward inside the bore and is propelled out of the muzzle with considerable velocity. The velocity may be subsonic or supersonic. The velocity of short-barrelled handguns is usually subsonic and often ranges from 600ft/sec to 1000ft/sec. For longer service or hunting rifled barrels, usually a supersonic high muzzle velocity is needed that often ranges from 2000 ft/sec to 3500 ft/sec. Based on velocity, firearms that are frequently encountered in crime may be differentiated as subsonic and supersonic velocity firearms, popularly known as low- and high-power firearms, respectively.

Variation in velocity is influenced by the rate of burning of the propellant, which in turn depends on the shape and size of the propellant. There exists a wide variation in the shapes and sizes of propellants to achieve degressive, progressive, sustained or fast rate of burning. It is apparent that the shape and size of the propellant is the most important factor for controlling the rate of burning in achieving the desired velocity. This may provide significant investigative leads in the absence of recovery of the firearm and/or ammunition. Square-shaped propellants fired from a short-barrelled auto pistol are shown in Figure 6.3.

In the absence of recovery of the firearm and ammunition, the shape and size of partially burnt or unburnt propellant particles found on the target may provide valuable clues about the probable type of firearm used – whether a high- or a low-velocity firearm. The expert may opine on the issue if the relevant exhibit is sent for forensic examination.

There is a wide variation in the shapes and sizes of propellants. They are usually flakes, in the form of discs and/or rectangular

Figure 6.3 Square-shaped propellants from a short-barrelled auto pistol

shapes, or solid cylindrical or tubular, ball powders, etc. Their rate of burning depends upon variation in their surface area because the propellant burns at the surface. The surface area of the burning solid cylindrical-shaped propellant continuously decreases, which makes it a degressive burning propellant. But the rate of burning varies differently with a tubular cylindrical form. Whereas the burning of the outer surface continuously decreases in tubular propellants, simultaneously, the burning of the inner surface continuously increases. This makes the all-burnt point of the propellant far beyond the breech near the muzzle end, thereby providing a sustained pressure on the forward-moving projectile, which helps in achieving a high emerging muzzle velocity. For fast-burning propellants, flakes in various shapes, such as square, circular discs, spherical, etc, are invariably used to provide a greater surface of burning in short-barrelled handguns that are low-velocity firearms.

7

Evidentiary values of firearms in criminal trials and investigative leads

Having familiarity with the evidentiary values of fired ammunition, one also needs to be familiar with the evidentiary values of the firearm that has been recovered from the suspect. The most significant investigative lead, therefore, relates to the search and seizure of the fired ammunition, an important component to establish or discard firearm–ammunition linkage.

We are aware that evidence bullet/bullet pieces are almost always found either in the victim's body or at the crime scene. Therefore, with the recovery of suspected firearm, it may always be possible to have an expert's positive, negative or inconclusive opinion about the linkage of the evidence fired projectile with the suspected firearm.

But it is not so with the fired empty, because it may or may not be found at the crime scene. It would essentially depend upon the way the empty is extracted and ejected after firing. If this is carried out manually, then the evidence empty may or may not be found at the crime scene. Alternatively, if both extraction and ejection are carried out by the action mechanism of the firearm, then the recovery of the evidence cartridge is almost certain at the crime scene. This necessitates familiarity with the functioning of the extractor and ejector of the firearm that was used in the commission of the crime. The action mechanism for the extraction and ejection of a fired empty varies widely from one type of firearm to another. This calls for classification of firearms. It is the sequence of firing operations that embraces all action mechanisms of a firearm which may be summarised as "load, lock, cock, fire, unlock, extract and eject." This proves helpful in providing varied investigating leads of forensic significance in addition to the search and seizure of fired ammunition.

DOI: 10.4324/9781351023863-9

The action mechanism of cocking, locking and firing operations provides investigative leads to assess whether the questioned firearm is prone to accidental fire in the hands of an unwary shooter.

Firearms that are frequently encountered in crime are pistols and revolvers, service and hunting rifles, carbines and assault rifles, shotguns and muzzle loaders, illegally made firearms including 3D printed guns, etc. They need to be classified to evaluate varied problems of forensic significance.

7.1 Classification of firearms

Foremost is the loading parameter which differentiates a vast majority of commonly met firearms in crime. They are manually operated, repeater and self-loading firearms.

7.1.1 Manually operated firearms and investigative leads

Firearms that are meant to load cartridges manually into the chamber are manually operated firearms. Extraction and ejection of the fired empties are also carried out manually (hence the name). Manually operated firearms that are frequently encountered in crimes are traditional single- or double-barrelled shotguns and multi-chambered revolvers. It is the variation in the functional parts of manually operated firearms that differentiates between multi-barrelled and multi-chambered firearms. The number of cartridges that can be loaded depends on the number of chambers or barrels it has.

7.1.1.1 Shotguns

The shotgun is a popular gun worldwide. It is a multipurpose gun. It is used for a variety of shooting sports and hunting. It is also used by enforcement agencies against rioters. It is the most sought-after firearms among civilians, especially in underdeveloped and developing countries, presumably because the licensing policy for possession of shotguns is comparatively liberal even in countries that enforce strict gun licensing policies. Their ammunition is also comparatively cheap and easily available. Besides branded factory-made ammunition, homemade shotgun cartridges are also common among game lovers.

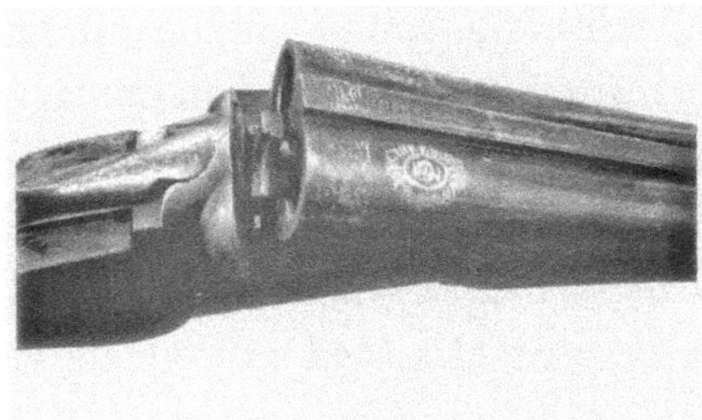

Figure 7.1 A 12-bore DBBL shotgun

Lead alloy shots, steel shots, wads, etc. are commercially available for homemade shotgun cartridges. Use of shotguns in criminal activities is also very common.

A shotgun is a smooth-bore shoulder firearm. It has a long barrel. The length of the barrel usually varies between 26 and 30 inches, although 18 inches is usually considered the minimum for classifying the firearm as shotgun. Commonly used shotguns in this category are single-barrelled and double-barrelled shotguns, popularly known as SBBL and DBBL guns, respectively.

Being a multipurpose firearm, the constructional features of shotgun barrels also vary considerably among smooth-bore shotguns of the same gauge/calibre. There may be wide variations in their chamber lengths, muzzle dimension and bore dimension.

a. Variation in chamber dimension

The number, size and weight of shots/pellets loaded in a shotgun cartridge vary with the multipurpose usage it has. Variation in load necessitates variation in the length of the cartridge. The most commonly used lengths of shotgun cartridges are 2½″/65mm, 2¾″/70mm and 3″/76mm. Variation in cartridge lengths necessitates variation in chamber lengths among shotguns of the same calibre. The chamber size of firearms varies with the varying cartridge lengths of 65mm, 70mm, 76mm, etc. that are in vogue. The chamber size is usually marked on shotguns and also on the walls of the cartridges.

Although the chamber size of a shotgun is designed to accommodate and fire cartridges of a specific length, it is usually possible to load mismatched cartridges into the chamber. Whereas a shorter-length cartridge can easily be loaded in a longer-chamber shotgun, it may also be possible to load a longer crimped cartridge into a shorter chamber size of the firearm – for example, a 2¾″ crimped cartridge can be loaded into a 2½″ chamber. However, it is not correct to assume that a cartridge that can be loaded in the firearm is always safe to fire. A longer cartridge in a small-size chamber squeezes the shots near the mouth which results in the development of higher pressure than the firearm is designed to sustain and is proofed for. This may at times be risky. One may also experience difficulty in the extraction and ejection of the fired empty. In either case, it influences the spread of pellets. Therefore, an expert can make an appropriate and approximate estimation of the probable range fire only if the evidence empty cartridge and the suspected firearm are available or the cartridge length and the chamber size of the suspected smooth-bore shotgun are known.

b. Variation in muzzle dimension – choke

The spread of pellets is an important aspect of shooting sports. Whereas a wide spread of pellets may be needed for one, a constricted spread may be needed for the other. Provision is made to constrict the spread of pellets before it emerges out of the muzzle. This is achieved by constricting the diameter at the muzzle end. This is known as choke. The constriction squeezes the column of travelling shots/pellets near the muzzle. This results in restricting the spread of pellets when they come out of the muzzle – the greater the constriction, the lesser is the spread of emerging pellets.

Figure 7.2 A six-chambered revolver

7.1.1.2 Revolvers

The revolver is primarily a firearm for self-defence and a popular companion among civilians, police and army personnel. It is a short-barrelled handgun and its barrel is rifled. The length of the barrel is usually less than 6 inches. It has a multi-chambered revolving cylinder to load and fire a number of cartridges without reloading. The cylinder is situated separately at the breech end of the barrel. It usually has provision to accommodate 5–7 cartridges. Revolvers with a six-chambered cylinder are very common. The cylinder of revolvers may rotate clockwise or anticlockwise depending on their make and model. The cocking and firing operations of revolvers are actuated by the hammer and trigger of the revolver.

a. Single-action and double-action revolvers

There are two types of revolvers, namely single-action and double-action revolvers. In the single-action revolver, cocking is done by pulling the hammer backwards, which rotates the cylinder to bring one of the loaded chambers in alignment with the barrel. The hammer is held back when it cocks the revolver to make it ready to fire. On pressing the trigger, the hammer falls and strikes the primer to initiate firing.

In double-action revolvers, a prolonged pull of the trigger performs both operations. It rotates the cylinder to bring the chamber in alignment with the barrel, cocks the firearm and fires the cartridge. There are double-action revolvers that can also be used as a single-action revolver. Double-action revolvers have the advantage of firing of cartridges by a single pull of the trigger for each fire until the cylinder is empty, and they are preferred for firing a number of rounds as a repeater without reloading. The only apparent drawback is a high trigger pull.

b. Trigger pull of revolvers

The trigger pull of about 15–16 lb is usually required to rotate the heavy cylinder to bring one of the chambers in alignment with the bore of the barrel and to cock the revolver. An additional trigger pull of about 3–4 lb is needed for actuating the trigger for the falling of the hammer to initiate the firing operation. This signifies that the trigger pull of a double-action revolver is approximately 20 lb as compared to

4–5 lb. for a single-action revolver. A heavy trigger pull is an important parameter in evaluating the act of suicide and struggle involving double-action revolvers.

7.1.2 Repeater firearms and investigative leads

A repeater firearm is virtually a manually operated firearm, except for the difference in loading operation. Instead of loading the cartridges manually into the chamber, in repeaters, they are fed into the chamber from a spring-loaded magazine which stores a number of rounds. This obviates the necessity of having multi-barrels/multi-chambers for firing more than one cartridge. The magazine is usually situated inside the stock or under the barrel and its capacity varies with the type of the firearm. Firearms that fall in the category of repeaters are usually bolt-action service and hunting rifles and pump-action shotguns.

> **Key note:** *The revolver is generally categorized as a repeater because it can fire repeatedly without reloading, although all firing operations including the loading of the cartridges are manually fed into the chambers of the rotating cylinder and not through a magazine.*

7.1.2.1 Bolt-action rifles

A rifle is primarily an anti-personnel weapon of soldiers for offence or defence. It is a shoulder firearm and its barrel is rifled. In bolt-action

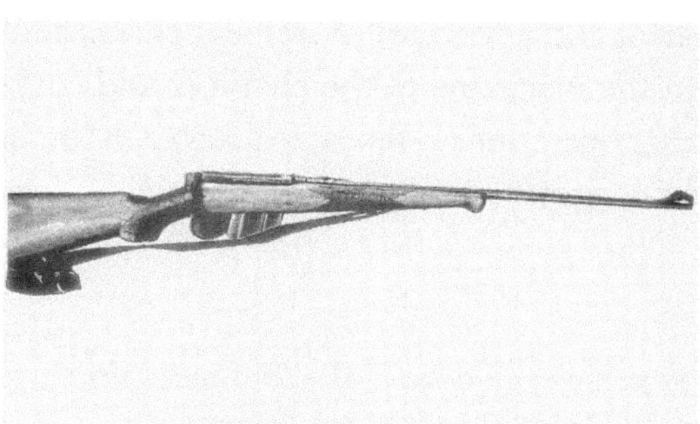

Figure 7.3 A .315 bolt-action rifle

rifles, the forward movement of the bolt takes a cartridge from the magazine which is fed into the chamber and cocks the firearm. After firing, the rearward movement of the bolt extracts and ejects the fired cartridge case, leaving the chamber empty to load another cartridge by the forward movement of the bolt. The most popular bolt-action service rifle of yesteryear is the Lee Enfield .303 bolt-action rifle having a magazine capacity of ten rounds. It is a high-powered firearm and its muzzle velocity is about 2,400 ft/sec. Bolt-action hunting rifles are popular among game hunters, and they are also high-powered firearms. Their muzzle velocity may be as high as 2,500 to 3,000 ft/sec and even beyond.

7.1.2.2 Pump-action shotguns

Another popular firearm in the category of repeaters is a pump-action shotgun. Pump-action shotguns are comparatively short-barrelled shotguns. They are used by enforcement agencies, generally used to control protestors and rioters. The one used by the police in India is a 18″ long-barrelled pump-action shotgun. Pump-action shotguns for civilian use have barrel length of 20″. It has a tubular magazine placed under the barrel that may store four to eight shotgun cartridges. It has a movable front forearm. The loading of live cartridges in the chamber and unloading of the fired cartridge empty out of the firearm are carried out by the movement of the front movable forearm. The forward movement of the movable forearm takes a cartridge from the tubular magazine, brings it into alignment with the chamber, loads the cartridge inside the chamber and cocks the firearm. After firing, the rearward movement of the forearm extracts and ejects the empty out of the firearm, and a forward movement thereafter loads another live round from the magazine to the chamber and cocks the firearm. The cycle of firing operations is repeated after each fire by pressing the trigger until the magazine is empty and there is no live round in the chamber.

7.1.3 Self-loading firearms (auto loaders) – semi-automatic and automatic firearms and investigative leads

In the present era, self-loading firearms are the most popular firearms. These are essentially magazine firearms. They utilise the power

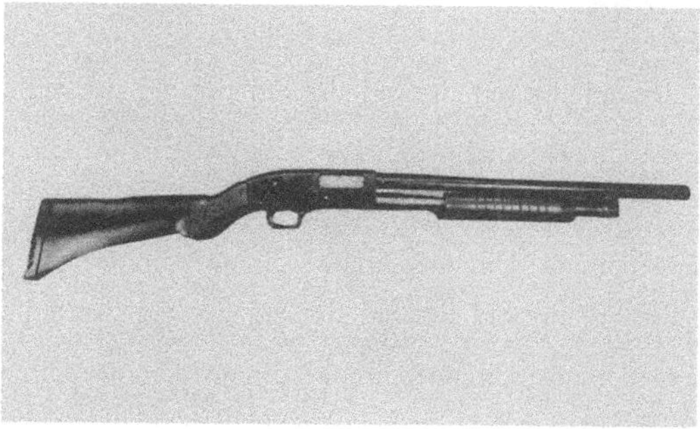

Figure 7.4 A 12-bore pump-action shotgun

of recoil, or a portion of the expanding gases to extract and eject the fired empty, and then load a live round in the chamber – hence the name, autoloaders or self-loading firearms. The most commonly used firearms in crimes in this category are self-loading pistols and assault rifles whose barrels are rifled.

7.1.3.1 Self-loading pistols

A self-loading pistol is also a self-defence firearm. It is a short-barrel handgun whose barrel length is usually less than 10 inches. It has a removable magazine housed inside a recess in the hand grip. Its spring-loaded magazine has the capacity to load about 8–10 cartridges. A slide containing the breech block moves to and fro over the barrel. On firing, the projectile and discharge residues are projected out of the muzzle and the slide is pushed backwards. It extracts and ejects the fired empty, takes a live round from the magazine, loads it into the chamber and cocks the trigger mechanism, thereby making it ready to fire again. This sequence is repeated by pressing the trigger after each fire until the magazine is empty and there is no live round left in the chamber.

Self-loading firearms are loosely termed automatic firearms. This is, however, a misnomer. In automatic firearms, the provision of continuous firing without releasing the trigger is made. Once the trigger of an automatic firearm is pressed, it will continue to fire until the magazine is empty or the trigger is released. Automatic firearms such as service rifles and machine guns are often used by police and military personnel. They attract strict legal provisions in arms laws. A self-loading firearm that requires the release of the trigger after

Figure 7.5 A 7.65mm semi-automatic pistol

each fire and for the trigger to be pressed afresh to fire the next round is a semi-automatic firearm. They include semi-automatic shotguns, pistols, rifles, etc.

7.1.3.2 Assault rifles

An assault rifle is essentially an autoloader usually capable of fully automatic fire. The Kalashnikov assault rifle, popularly known as the AK47, is the most popular firearm in the world. It is lightweight and easy to use and maintain. It has a detachable banana-shaped magazine that can load 30 cartridges. It can fire both as a semi-automatic as well as a fully automatic firearm. The AK47 has been adopted as service rifles by several countries. It is believed that more than 80 million AK47-type assault rifles have been manufactured worldwide by various countries. There are various models/variants such as the AK56, AK74, etc. Modern variants are often referred as AKMs (assault Kalashnikov moderns). A recent model/variant is the AK203, which is being manufactured in India. It is designed to fire 1,000 rounds per minute. In addition, there are other improved features in the AK203.

The family of AK47 rifles is also comparatively inexpensive and easily available in the grey market. Its automatic rapid fire and detachable magazine capacity of 30 rounds make it a weapon of choice for the terrorist and mass killer. It is the AR-15 that is the most popular assault rifle in the USA. Both the AK 47 and AR-15 assault rifles are used by military and the police force as well. Being fully automatic firearms, their use for self-defence and other criminal activities attract legal implications in arms legislation.

Figure 7.6 An AK47 assault rifle

7.2 Firearms as evidentiary clues for search and seizure of fired empty

A combined reading of the mechanism of the functioning of the extractor and ejector of manually operated, repeater and gas-operated firearms clearly reveals that:

- It may not be necessary to empty the chamber of the firearm that requires manual unloading of the fired empty after committing the crime of firing at the victim. Firearms that fall in this category are traditional shotguns (SBBL/DBBL guns), single-shot bolt-action rifles and multi-chambered revolvers. Unless the firearm is reloaded for firing more cartridges than the firearm is designed to accommodate, the assailant does not remove the empty which may be carried along with the firearm after committing the crime. In such cases, the empty is recovered from the possession or at the instance of the accused. It may not be recovered if it is destroyed. This is equally true for repeater firearms having a magazine, such as rifles and pump-action shotguns, if only one round is fired in the criminal incident of fire. However, the maximum number of fired empties that the assailant can carry depends upon the number of barrels/chambers the suspect firearm has, to accommodate and to fire. A DBBL shotgun having double barrel can load and fire two cartridges and a six-chambered revolver can load and fire six cartridges as a repeater.
- It becomes necessary to remove the fired empty from the chamber if the firearm is reloaded to keep armed for a subsequent eventuality or to fire more rounds. In such cases, fired empties are invariably found at the place of criminal incidents of gunfire. It is the empty of the last round that the assailant

may carry along with the firearm. The number of fired empties found at the crime scene may not necessarily correspond to the number of rounds fired in the criminal incident of gunfire.

Empties are necessarily thrown out of repeater firearms if more than one round is fired. In such cases also, the number of empties at the crime scene would correspond to the number of fires if the last empty is also extracted and ejected to empty the chamber.

It is only in cases of auto loaders that the empties are automatically extracted and ejected out of the firearm at the place of occurrence of gunfire crime. In such cases, the number of empties at the crime scene corresponds to the number of fires.

Having familiarity with the aforementioned evidentiary values of firearms, fired ammunition and their investigative leads, one is fully equipped for an effective investigation of the truthfulness of eyewitness and suspect versions on a scientific basis.

8

Eyewitness statements and investigative leads

The role of an investigator primarily begins with the preliminary investigation of the victim or the eyewitness who reports the criminal incident of gunfire. The witness narrates the details of the sequence of shooting incidents. It stands as statement of facts unless proved otherwise. This forms the basis for initiation of investigation of the criminal incident. The investigator is therefore required to derive investigative leads of oral and physical evidence from the statement of eyewitness.

8.1 Statement on firing at the victim for investigative leads of physical clues

The eyewitness usually provides a fairly clear description of firing that caused death or grievous/simple injuries to the victim. In the absence of requisite information, the following non-technical queries may prove helpful in assessing the possible physical clues and investigative leads:

a. Whether it was a fire from close or distant range and whether the portion of the body that was hit was bare or clothed. *This helps in identifying the probable site for the presence or absence of close-range firearm discharge.*
b. Whether it was a single or multiple projectile hits that caused single or multiple injuries. *This helps in identifying the number of fires and type of firearm.*
c. Whether the victim suffered minor or grievous injury causing death. *This help in identifying the wounding capability of the firearm at a specified range.*

The investigating officer is required to provide immediate medical help to the injured victim. The victim who dies before or after medical help

DOI: 10.4324/9781351023863-10

is sent for post-mortem examination. The medical officer/autopsy surgeon attending the victim examines the firearm injuries and recovers lodged fired bullets or bullet pieces, pellets and plastic or cardboard wads or wad pieces. These are handed over to the investigating officer in sealed packets along with the post-mortem or medico-legal injury report. The victim's clothing and sometimes even skin cuttings bearing bullet/pellet holes and firearm discharge are also handed over to the investigating officer. The physical clues so recovered from the victim's body provide investigative leads for significant forensic conclusions in connecting the crime with the criminal weapon and the criminal. For this purpose, the sealed packets containing the bullet/bullet pieces and the victim's clothing or skin cuttings are required to be forwarded to the forensic laboratory for expert opinion on the following:

- To opine on the calibre, make and model of the suspected rifled firearm from the bullet/bullet pieces that were recovered from the injured/dead victim. This will help in the search for the involved rifled firearm, eliminating the improbable.
- To opine on the bore of the shotgun from the wad that was recovered from the victim.
- To opine on the bullet hole on the clothing/skin cuttings, whether created by the passage of jacketed or unjacketed bullets.
- To opine on the presence or absence of close-range firearm discharge on the clothing of the victim and on the skin cuttings of the victim and probable range of fire.

Key note: *If the eyewitness statement signifies close-range firing, then it becomes obligatory on the part of investigating officer to ensure that there is specific mention of the presence of close-range phenomena such as singeing, charring, blackening or powder tattooing in the medico-legal or post-mortem report. Its absence in the report may adversely affect the corroboration of close-range firing on a scientific basis and the merit of the case. Similarly, this is equally true, if there is specific mention of close-range phenomena in the injury/post-mortem report but the eyewitness specifically mentions distant fire much beyond the generally accepted concept of close range.*

8.2 Statement on functioning of the firearm during firing incidents and investigative leads

This information provides valuable investigative leads. But it is often missed in the eyewitness statement, presumably because of lack of knowledge about the firearm. If so, this information needs to be sought. The following non-technical queries may prove helpful in assessing the requisite information and consequent investigative leads for physical clues:

- Whether the firearm was ejecting empties automatically. *This identifies the recovery of physical clues at the place of the shooting incident and the use of autoloaders or repeaters, eliminating others.*
- Whether the firearm was a shoulder or a handgun. *This helps in the investigation of involved firearm, eliminating the improbable.*
- Whether the firearm was firing single bullets/multiple projectiles. *This identifies the type of firearm, whether rifled firearm or shotgun.*
- Whether the empties were ejected manually. *This identifies the use of a non-self-loading firearm or repeater and likely physical clues at the place of shooting incident.*
- Whether fresh cartridges were loaded after one, two or more fires. *This identifies the number of fires and physical clues of fired empties at the place of shooting incident.*

The above information equips the investigating officer to identify the course of investigation in terms of what needs to be collected as evidentiary clues at the place of the shooting incident. A detailed account of the place of the criminal incident of gunfire is always narrated by the eyewitness.

8.3 Place of occurrence of criminal incident of gunfire (the where) and investigative leads

This investigative lead of the eyewitness about the place of shooting incident is highly significant for the recovery of the physical evidence for connecting the crime with the criminal weapon. The place of shooting incident may be:

a. the house of the victim
b. the house of the accused

c. a public place such as busy marketplace, movie hall, sports stadium
d. a social gathering such as marriages, religious and political functions, demonstrations
e. remote places such as lanes and roads, empty parks, deserted ground.

The enforcement agency seals the place of occurrence as early as possible after the crime is reported so that the crime scene is not disturbed until the requisite investigation is completed. The chances of a disturbed crime scene are very high at social gatherings and busy public places. Exact locations of the physical clues in such cases may be misleading. At times, the physical evidence may even be missing. These aspects need to be borne in mind while reconstructing the crime scene.

The evidentiary clues that are likely to be found at the place of the criminal incident are the fired empties, fired bullets/bullet pieces, fired pellets, and fired wads that did not hit the victim or exited after entering the body. Their respective locations help in reconstructing the crime scene.

The firearm is very rarely found at the crime scene unless the assailant is apprehended during or after firing at the victim. It remains invariably with the assailant until the investigating agency apprehends the suspect and recovers the firearm. If the place of occurrence of the crime happens to be the house of the suspect/accused, the recovery of the firearm is usually possible.

8.4 Statement on date and time of shooting incident (the when) and investigative leads

The date and time of the criminal incident of gunfire is an important record of the first information report (FIR). The eyewitness invariably gives a detailed account about the specific hour of the day when the crime took place. This provides investigative leads about the visibility during the commission of the crime, a determinant factor of witnessing and narrating the true criminal incident. Factors that often influence visibility, in addition to the specific hours of the day, are change of weather, season or brightness of the light, as evinced from the following:

a. variable visibility hours of the day: morning, noon, evening or night
b. variable weather: sunny day (clear visibility), rainy/snowy day (poor visibility)
c. variable season: summer, winter or spring (darkness occurs early in winter)
d. broad daylight or bright evening lights (clear visibility)
e. dark night (impaired visibility).

An assessment of the truthfulness of the eyewitness statement for identification of the assailant is possible if visibility during the criminal incidence of gunfire is clear. In the event of poor visibility, witnessing the criminal incident is a difficult task and it may not be possible to identify correctly even a known assailant. It may lead to the mistaken identity of the suspect/accused.

8.5 Statement on identifying the perpetrator of the crime (the who) and recovery of firearms

The identities of the assailant and victim are often known to the eyewitness who reports the shooting incident. It may not be known if the witness is a passer-by or a stranger. In case of cross-firing between the two rival parties, the identity of assailants and victims may or may not be known to the eyewitnesses of either party who report the shooting incident.

Once the assailant is identified and apprehended, it is usually possible to recover the firearm. It is either surrendered or is recovered at the instance of the accused. The firearm, recovered along with the physical exhibits that had been seized at the crime scene, is forwarded to the expert for opinion on all possible issues that are relevant to the crime, especially on the following:

a. whether the firearm attracts the provisions of the arms legislation of the land
b. whether the firearm had been recently discharged

c. whether the seized fired empties and bullets had been fired from the recovered firearm.

8.5.1 Mistaken identity of the perpetrator of the crime

Sometimes, there may be mistaken identity of the perpetrator of the crime. This is usually due to physical ailment/deficiencies of the eyewitness such as poor eyesight, old age, etc. Besides physical ailment/deficiencies, the most important factor that influences mistaken identity of the assailant is poor visibility during the criminal incident of the gunfire.

8.5.1.1 Poor visibility and mistaken identity of assailant

While discussing visibility, the Supreme Court of India in the case *Ram Narain Singh v. State of Punjab* (1975) held:

> On the day of the occurrence i.e. October 2, 1972, it would be quite dark at 8-00 P.M. [...] The evidence of some of the witnesses unmistakably points in the conclusion that the occurrence really took place at 8 P.M. when it was dark, and if that is so, then there is no evidence on the record to show how the appellant could have been identified by the witnesses. [...] [I]f the occurrence took place at 8-00 P.M. the possibility of mistake in identification cannot be excluded in the present circumstances [...] It is obvious that where the direct evidence is not supported by the expert evidence, then the evidence is wanting in the most material part of the prosecution case and it would be difficult to convict the accused on the basis of such evidence. [...] For the reasons given above we were satisfied that the prosecution had not been able to prove its case against any of the accused beyond reasonable doubt and the appellants were, therefore, entitled to an acquittal.

Visibility during the firing incident therefore forms a crucial determining factor for wrong identity of the assailant.

8.5.1.2 Fairly similar features and mistaken identity of assailant

In addition to physical ailment and visibility, the fairly similar features of two or more persons may lead to mistaken identity of the assailant. This may lead to even wrongful conviction. This is especially so if the suspect is not known to the eyewitness.

An unusual criminal case of mistaken identity and wrong conviction has been cited in a paper titled "Evaluating eyewitness testimony in criminal trials" by Maureen A. Gorman, published in *Chicago-Kent Law Review* (1987). In the instant case, the suspect Ronald Quick was tried twice in Kansas courts for robbery of a liquor store. At both trials, two eyewitnesses positively identified Quick as the perpetrator of the crime. Quick was convicted at both trials. However, both conviction orders were reversed as trial errors, when another man who looked like Quick confessed to the crime during the third trial.

8.6 Statement on motive or reason for firing at the victim (the why) and investigative leads

The reason or motive for firing is important information as it substantiates or rejects the act of criminal intent of the assailant. The motive for committing a crime is invariably included in the statement of the witness if both assailant and victim are known to the witness. Motive acts as strong corroborative evidence. It is an important factor that weighs most when the evidence against the defendant is entirely circumstantial and there is no eyewitness. Although due importance is attributed to the motive of committing the crime, it is not the only criteria on the basis of which a conviction can be awarded. It depends upon the merit of other evidence as well, especially if these are reliable and trustworthy to prove the guilt of the accused. The following court judgments in respect of motive are worth mentioning.

While discussing failure of the prosecution to prove motive, the Supreme Court of India in the case *Nachhttar Singh v. State of Punjab* (1975) has held:

> Be that as it may, the failure of the prosecution to establish the motive for the crime does not mean that the entire prosecution case has to be thrown over-board. It only casts a duty on the Court to scrutinise the other evidences, particularly of the eyewitnesses, with greater care. The High Court was fully conscious of the need for such caution, and rightly observed: "The absence of proof of motive has this effect only that the other evidence bearing on the guilt of the accused has to be very carefully examined." Indeed, the High Court did so. The conviction of the appellant mainly rests on the evidence of Bhagwan Kaur, PW 2 which

> had been corroborated in material particulars by independent evidence, including that of the Ballistic Expert, Mr J.K Sinha.

In the case *Evans v. Commonwealth* (1929), the court held:

> Proof of motive is not a matter without which a conviction cannot be had. In Marcum vs. Com., 1 S.W. 727, 8 Ky. Law Rep. 418, the defendant was appealing from a sentence of death. This court affirmed the judgment, and, in the opinion, commented on the utter absence of evidence of motive. Society is but little interested in why Evans killed Chief Woolum, except as such evidence of why he did it may tend to throw light upon the main question, which was, did he do it? The jury has said he did. No improper evidence was adduced before it. It was correctly instructed. The trial was orderly conducted, the evidence supports the verdict, and the judgment entered thereon is affirmed.

While discussing firing at the victim without reason or motive, the Supreme Court of India in the case *Raj Kumar v. State of Haryana* (1996) held:

> The gun which was recovered from the accused and empties which were recovered from the spot were sent for analysis to the ballistic expert. Although it was reported that the gun was in working condition and the cartridge cases lifted from the place were held to have been fired from the gun, but it was of no use as it did not corroborate the prosecution case. Further evidence of eyewitnesses was wholly inconsistent with medical evidence, and it was difficult to accept them as eyewitnesses to occurrence. *There was no motive on the part of the accused to kill deceased* and evidence of other witnesses was contradictory to each other. Therefore, there was no cogent evidence to support prosecution case.

The conviction was set aside and the appellant was acquitted.

9

Investigation of Admitted Firing in Criminal Trials

9.1 Accidental fire – no motive, reason or intent to fire at the victim

One often comes across cases of accidental firing. This is usually due to the mishandling of a firearm, mainly because of a lack of basic understanding of the cycle of firing operation, especially the loading, firing and unloading operations of cartridges/empties which vary from one type of firearm to the other and sometime even from one model to the other. A firearm in the hands of an unwary person is very dangerous. Such a person is usually tempted to press the trigger without knowing whether the firearm is loaded or not. This often results in accidental fire that may cause death or grievous/simple injuries to the victim. Such a lapse is also likely from a person having limited or superficial knowledge. The investigating officer must ensure that the firearm recovered during investigation from the possession or at the instance of the accused or otherwise is not handled by any person, even by assisting investigation staff, unless live rounds/fired empties, if any, are removed.

The investigating officer is also required to ensure that under no circumstances is a loaded firearm forwarded to the ballistic expert for an opinion on accidental fire. To unload a live round and fired empty, one needs to be conversant with their locations in the functional part of the firearm and with the functioning of the firearm in question to make it safe before forwarding to the expert.

The following investigative aspects needs to be addressed in cases of accidental fire.

DOI: 10.4324/9781351023863-11

9.2 Deceptive perception of empty magazine and accidental fire

Autoloader and repeater firearms have spring-loaded magazines that house live rounds one over the other. The number of rounds that can be loaded in the magazine depends upon the type of firearm. Cartridges are fed into the chamber from the magazine for firing one after the other. In autoloaders, the fired empty is extracted and ejected by the backward gases after each fire, and another live round is loaded into the chamber from the magazine and cocked, ready to fire. Repeater firearms, having magazines, are usually bolt-action firearms. After each fire, the cartridge empty is extracted and ejected, and a fresh live cartridge is loaded into the chamber by manual rearward and forward bolt operation. Live cartridges are fed into the chamber until live rounds are available in the magazine both in autoloaders and repeaters. After the last round is fed into the chamber, the magazine becomes empty. The last round in the chamber held in the cocked position makes the firearm ready to fire. An empty magazine provides a deceptive perception to an unwary person that the firearm is not loaded, and they may be tempted to press the trigger, causing accidental fire. It is therefore necessary that not only the magazine but also the chamber needs to be verified for a live round. Unless so verified, the firearm poses a serious threat in the hands of an unwary person.

An empty magazine does not necessarily signify that it is not a loaded auto pistol/repeater. The magazine is emptied after the last round is loaded in the chamber, but the chamber is not emptied until the last round is fired.

9.2.1 Direction of rotating cylinder and accidental fire

One often comes across cases of accidental firing by double-action revolvers. This is usually due to the mishandling of a firearm because of a lack of basic understanding of the direction of rotation of the cylinder of the revolver. The cylinder of a revolver may rotate clockwise or anticlockwise depending on make and model. If only one live cartridge is loaded on the right or on the left side of the cylinder, whether it will fire or not upon pressing the trigger will depend upon the direction of rotation of the cylinder. Ignorance about the direction of rotation of the firearm in hand may result in accidental fire. The live cartridge on the right side of the cylinder of a revolver having anticlockwise rotation would fire the cartridge by pressing the trigger, but it will not fire the live cartridge if the cylinder rotates clockwise. The loaded chamber will move farther in the right direction. Likewise, a loaded chamber on the left will result in firing of the cartridge on pressing the trigger if the cylinder rotates clockwise. *A trigger-happy handler, unaware of the direction of rotation of the cylinder, may accidentally fire the revolver, resulting in grievous injury or even death to the victim.*

9.2.2 Lighter trigger pull and accidental fire

The trigger pull of firearms that are commonly met in crimes is usually 3–5 lb; it is 16–20 lb for double-action revolvers and is an important parameter to assess whether the firearm is prone to accidental fire. However, for all practical purposes one can assume that the lighter the trigger pull, the more is the weapon prone to accidental discharge. Firearms having very light trigger pull are prone to accidental fire even by falling on the floor or due to heavy jerk.

9.3 Admitted firing in self-defence

The right to private (self-) defence is recognized worldwide. There have been monumental court judgments that have outlined the guiding principles relating to private rights to protect life and property.

Way back in 1921, in the Supreme Court of United States of America, in the case *Brown v. United States*, Justice Homes ruled on the guiding principles of the right to private (self-) defence. The significant ones are:

- "Detached reflection cannot be demanded in the presence of an uplifted knife." A person in fear of his life is not expected to modulate his defence step by step or tier by tier.
- "If a man reasonably believes that he is in immediate danger of death or grievous bodily harm from his assailant, he may stand his ground [and] if he kills him, he has not exceeded the bounds of lawful self-defense."

In India, the law relating to private defence is governed by Section 96 of the India Penal Code (IPC) which states that nothing is an offence which is done in the exercise of the right to private defence. Section

97 of the IPC provides that a right to private defence extends not only to the defence of one's own body against any offence affecting the human body but also to the defence of the body of any other person. The right also embraces the protection of property, whether one's own or another person's, against certain specified offences, namely, theft, robbery, mischief and criminal trespass.

In 2010, the Supreme Court of India outlined the principles of right to private (self-)defence in case *Darshan Singh v. State of Punjab* (2010). The significant guiding principles held by the court are:

- The right to private defence is available only to one who is suddenly confronted with the necessity of averting an impending danger and not one of self-creation.
- It is unrealistic to expect a person under assault to modulate his defence step by step with any arithmetical exactitude.
- The right to private defence commences as soon as a reasonable apprehension arises. It is not necessary that there should be an actual commission of the offence.
- A person who is in imminent and reasonable danger of losing life or limb may, in exercise of self-defence, inflict any harm even extending to death of his assailant either when the assault is attempted or directly threatened.
- It is well settled that even if the accused does not plead self-defence, such a plea may be considered if the same arises from the material on record.
- The accused need not prove the existence of the right to private defence beyond reasonable doubt.

9.3.1 Self-defence to save life of fellow officer and reliable eyewitness

The case *Ronnie G. Clark v. State of Louisiana* (2003) exemplifies the justification for firing at an aggressor to protect the life of fellow officer while discharging their official duties. A convicted felon on parole was involved in a high-speed chase while riding his motorcycle. The police set up a roadblock. The felon tried to run over the roadblock, coming straight at one of the state troopers directly in his line of travel. Both the troopers felt threatened and resorted to firing at the felon, paralyzing him from the waist down. The defence put forward the plea that the state troopers were unjustified in their use of force which went beyond what was necessary to protect a fellow police officer who was in danger of getting harmed.

While discussing the role of the two police officers on duty in resorting to firing at the victim, the court, relying on the testimony of the lay witness, held that the plaintiff was the aggressor and his actions led to reasonable fear that a fellow law enforcement officer was in the danger of death or bodily harm and the use of deadly force by both was reasonably necessary under the circumstances.

9.3.2 Right to self-defence and expert evidence

There is a very thin line dividing self-defence and cold-blooded murder, and the courts may need detailed information to correctly reconcile between witness testimony and scientific evidence. The Supreme Court of India stressed that circumstances are key in determining right to self-defence. While exonerating a Border Security Force constable for justifiably exercising the right by firing at a group of smugglers who has closed in on his outpost at the Indo-Bangladesh border, killing a notorious smuggler, the court held that: "The right to self-defense would be available to the accused when he or his property is faced with a danger and there is little scope of the state machinery coming to his aid." Rejecting the findings of the General Security Force Court and the High Court that it was a cold-blooded murder, the Supreme Court of India in the case *EX. CT. Mahadev v DG BSF* (2002) held:

> Trajectory of the bullets indicates the firing took place from a higher position vis-à-vis the deceased. That does not necessarily mean that the appellant had summoned the deceased and made him crouch on the ground before shooting him. The uneven terrain of rubber plantation with slopes and undulating surface would offer a plausible alternative explanation for the trajectory of bullets fired at the deceased.

9.3.3 Grudge against victim and misuse of right to self-defence

In the case *Bhupenrasinh v. State of Gujarat* (1997), despite being acquitted by all lower courts, the Supreme Court held a contrarian view on the basis of additional evidence and sentenced the appellant for the cold-blooded murder of his superior.

The appellant shot his superior while he was doing rounds around a dam site during the hours of dusk on a cloudy day. The appellant claimed that it was dark, and he saw a flame near the tower and someone moving; despite the appellant calling out to stop, the person did not and the appellant shot him in self-defence to protect the government property.

The court took particular note of the circumstances that the appellant was nurturing a grudge against the deceased. The post-mortem found that the wounds indicated close-range fire based on the blackening of the skin around two entry wounds.

The court held:

> Appellant put forward a case for right of private defense only when he was examined by the trial court under Section 313 of the code. High Court has noted that the has not disclosed to any of the prosecution witnesses that the was unable to identify his immediate superior and thought him to be a miscreant and observed that "no such question with regard to the mistaken identity was put to any other prosecution witnesses during the cross-examination." On the other hand, PW-12 (another SRP personnel who was also on duty) has deposed that he saw the appellant scampering away from the scene of occurrence and that when he was confronted he blurted out that he was proceeding to surrender himself since he had fired at the deceased. To none the appellant said that they fired the rifle to protect the tower. To none he disclosed that the first had a glimpse of flame which he thought to be the movement of a miscreant, In fact when the dead body and the surroundings were closely examined by the police they did not come across any material which could have given any mistaken impression to the appellant as flame of a torch. Thus, the belated claim of right of private defense was far from the contemplation of the appellant when he opened the fire at the deceased.
>
> In the light of the aforesaid discussion there is no scope to conclude that appellant had any right of private defence to property. Accordingly, we confirm the conviction and sentence and dismiss the appeal.

9.4 Admitted firing in the air to celebrate an occasion

Firing in the air is very common to celebrate an occasion, to disburse a crowd and or to scare. In India, special occasions for firing in air are usually marriage ceremonies, winning elections and sports matches, and even parties. Shotguns loaded with smaller pellets are the most popular, although handguns and other types are also used. It appears that there is common belief that firing in air will not cause harm to the crowded participants. A theoretical calculation of the terminal energy of shots/pellets falling from sufficient height (Jauhari & Sinha, 1962) has revealed that smaller shot and pellets including single ball are not expected to cause disabling wounds if 58 ft/lb is taken as the threshold energy for the same. This holds good if the firearm is fired vertically upwards, but if fired at an angle, the results may be different depending on the angle of fire. This is especially so if handguns or other firearms are involved, causing even death. In marriage ceremonies especially in north India, it is usually considered a matter of pride to fire in the air to show jubilation during the marriage procession to the wedding venue. In one such case, *State v. Jasbir Chauhan* (2015), the bridegroom's friend, despite being repeatedly told to desist from firing in the marriage procession, took out his licensed pistol and fired two shots in the air. A family member of the participant became the victim of firing in the air, which resulted in his death. But the defence took refuge in the argument that there were others in the wedding party who had fired their weapons. Since the witnesses were part of the same wedding party, they too became hostile and supported the defendant's claim.

The court, in view of the opinion of the ballistic expert that the bullet recovered from the body of the victim was fired from the pistol, coupled with the corroborating evidence of firing from the marriage video that was being simultaneously filmed at the time of fire, held the appellant guilty and was convicted.

PART III

Scientific Aspects in Criminal Trials Involving Firearms

Identification of firearms from fired ammunition

The scientific aspect of identification of a firearm from fired ammunition in criminal trials is highly significant. The fundamental principles, scientific methodologies adopted for the examination and comparison of test and evidence ammunition, interpreting the results of examination and forming of opinion are well known. These aspects have also been dealt with in the preceding sections in varied contexts. It is a routine examination carried out by scientific experts of firearm/ballistics unit of a forensic laboratory. The expert's opinion helps the court in making a judicious decision; if it is considered trustworthy and infallible, it is a must in the present scenario of the criminal justice system which has placed the science of forensic firearm identification at the crossroads. This calls for identifying issues that need to be

DOI: 10.4324/9781351023863-12

taken care of and evolving plausible modifications in the examination procedures to make the opinion devoid of error as far as practicable. Identification procedures for fired empties and fired bullets are separately discussed, incorporating ways to minimize error in all issues so identified to achieve an almost zero-error opinion.

10

IDENTIFICATION OF FIREARMS FROM FIRED EMPTIES

The procedure for identifying firearms from fired empties is well known. To begin with, it is necessary to obtain repeatable characteristic marks on the test-fired empties to ascertain the identifying features of the firearm. This is ensured if the test-fired empties bear clear identifiable surface profiles of the identifying parts of the firearm such as firing pin, breech, extractor and ejector that are imprinted on the base and that of the chamber on the walls of the test-fired empties.

The factors that influence clarity of identifying marks are as follows.

10.1 Interfering marks on test cartridges

Interfering marks that are very common are due to mishandling of the cartridge at various stages before and after firing.

i. Though uncommon but not rare, one finds the monogram of the manufacturing company embossed on the primer, which often interferes with the identifying marks of the firearm, especially the firing pin marks as shown in Figure 10.1.

Figure 10.1 Monogram of ICI embossed on the primer

DOI: 10.4324/9781351023863-13

ii. One also finds, though very rarely, prominent marks produced during the manufacturing processes of the cartridge.

These marks may mask prominent and clear impressions of the identifying features of the firearm. This may pose problems not only in ascertaining the identifying features of the firearm but also in forming opinions on comparison with the marks on the evidence empty. To obviate such a possibility, the expert must scrutinize live cartridges before test-firing to discover whether prominent interfering marks are present. If so, such cartridges should not be used for test purposes even if they are deemed preferred, being cartridges of same make, lot and batch as that of the evidence empty. This is one of the most important criteria for the imprinting of clear comparable identifying features of the firearm on test empties without significant interfering marks.

10.2 Clarity of marks on test cartridges

10.2.1 Hardness of the metal of the primer

The hardness of the metal of the primer is another parameter for the clarity of marks of the firing pin hit. The indentation of the firing pin hit on a softer surface is more pronounced than a harder metal surface of the primer. The softer the metal of the primer, the clearer the firing pin hit marks are. The metal of the primer should be neither very soft nor very hard. It should neither be so soft that the firing pin hit perforates the primer and creates a hole nor so hard that the firing pin hit becomes ineffective to initiate the firing process, resulting in misfires and hang fires.

10.2.2 Development of pressure

Development of pressure is the most important factor for the imprinting of breech marks. The higher the pressure developed, the clearer the impressions of breech marks are. At times, one has to fire a number of test rounds to obtain identifiable clear breech marks; the same is true for chamber marks. The firing pin indentation also becomes more pronounced by the backward force of the cartridge case after the pressure is generated on firing. This results in enhancing the clarity of firing pin impressions.

10.2.3 Striker blow

A hard striker blow on the primer imprints clearer impressions of the firing pin compared to a relatively weaker striker blow. A very hard striker blow on a soft metal of the primer may perforate the primer.

These factors may prove helpful in making an appropriate choice of test cartridges for evaluating identifying features of the firearm. This will help in minimizing error on this count.

10.3 Misleading examination and comparison of marks

Having discovered the identifying features of the firearm, these need to be compared with those available on the evidence empty to ascertain whether they are similar in order to arrive at a positive opinion or otherwise. Ordinarily, this is a thumb rule well known to the experts. But does it hold good in the preset era of rapidly changing crime pattern? Certainly not! And the reason is obvious. Criminals of today, in the modern era of science and technology, are very aware of the scientific methodologies adopted for the linkage of fired ammunition with the suspected firearm and that a positive opinion would provide strong support to connect the crime with the weapon of offence. As the accused ordinarily does not part with the firearm – unless apprehended while committing the crime – there remains ample opportunity to make all possible attempts to tamper with the firearm to evade detection until it is surrendered or seized by enforcement agencies. The consequent fallout is unprecedented; the ever-changing criminal modus operandi poses varied problems in forming a correct opinion. Even the rule of positive, negative and no-definite opinion may not hold good. The expert of today needs to be aware of this ever-changing modus operandi being used to evade detection and exercise due caution when forming and testifying opinion.

10.3.1 Criminal modus operandi to evade detection

10.3.1.1 Replace the firing pin

In a criminal case, the firing pin of the shotgun was replaced after the crime was committed. The gun was then surrendered. As expected, the firing pin marks of the surrendered gun did not tally with the firing pin marks on the seized evidence cartridge. Based on the basic principles of the evaluation of marks, the only opinion that could possibly be formed would be that the said cartridge had *not* been fired from the suspected gun. But is that a correct opinion? Obviously not. It would also be incorrect to opine that the cartridge had been fired from the suspected gun and so also that it is not possible to form definite opinion due to insufficient marks. In such a case, the expert has to exercise great caution and to form not only a correct opinion but also a guarded opinion so that justice may not be impaired. Hence:

i. In the absence of any other identifiable marks, the only opinion that can be formed is that the firing pin marks on the evidence empty do not tally with the firing pin marks of the suspected firearm.
ii. In addition to different firing pin marks, if any other identifiable marks produced by the development of pressure – such as breech marks, chamber marks, etc. – are available on the evidence empty that match with the suspected firearm, then one can safely conclude that the evidence empty had been fired from the firearm, despite different firing pin marks as shown in Figure 10.2.
iii. One may safely form a negative opinion only if additional identifiable marks that are produced by the development of pressure, if available, also do not match with the marks of the suspected firearm besides non-matching firing pin marks.

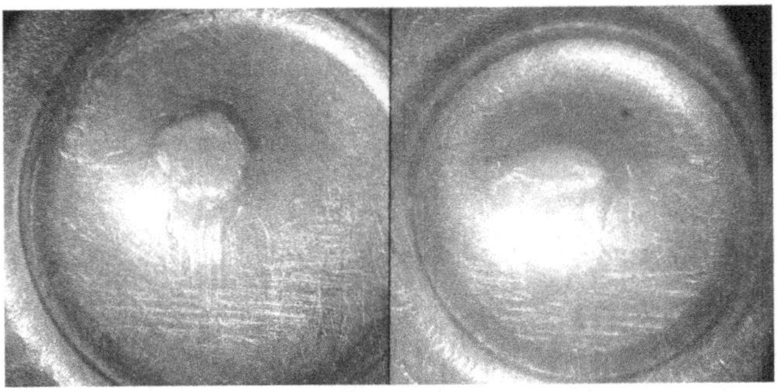

Figure 10.2 Different firing pin marks but similar breech

Thus, there may be three plausible opinions, depending upon additional identifiable marks that are produced by the development of pressure, whether matching or not matching with the suspect firearm.

10.3.1.2 Tamper with the firing pin

There have been criminal cases in which the firing pin had been tampered with by filing either wholly or partly. Firing pins of traditional SBBL and DBBL guns, bolt-action single or repeater firearms and revolvers having hinged barrels can easily be tampered with. In the absence of other identifying marks, the act of tampering with the firing pin must form part of the opinion due to which a definite opinion could not be formed despite different firing pin impressions on the test and evidence empty.

Deceptive simultaneous similar and dissimilar marks

In the case of a firing pin that has been partly tampered with, one may expect both similar as well as dissimilar firing pin impressions compared to the firing pin impressions present on the evidence fired empty. This ambiguity can be sorted out by examining the firing pin. It is usually possible to detect the tampering of the firing pin. The presence of shining striations due to filing often confirms the tampering. One must opine on the intentional act of tampering due to which a definite opinion could not be formed. In addition to firing pin marks, if identifiable marks that are produced by the development of pressure – such as breech and/or chamber – are present on the evidence empty, then one can safely infer a positive opinion if they are similar and a negative opinion if dissimilar. As tampering provides strong corroborative proof of the guilt of the accused, it must form a part of the expert's opinion.

10.3.1.3 Make the firearm unserviceable

Attempts are made to make the firearm unserviceable so that test cartridges and bullets cannot be fired for the purpose of comparison and opinion. There have been cases of bent barrels and breaking of the parts of the firearm into a number of pieces. The expert, in such cases, has no alternative but to either remain non-committal or to make sincere efforts to form an opinion by modifying the usual identifying procedures. In cases where test cartridges cannot be fired, the imprinting of identifying marks can easily be obtained on a softer lead surface by applying far less pressure. It must be understood that it is only necessary to obtain the impressions of the identifying parts of the firearm for comparison with the marks on the evidence empty and forming of opinion; it is immaterial as to how it has been obtained. The necessity of employing other means for obtaining the required impressions in view of attempts to make the firearm unserviceable, to evade detection, supports the guilt of the accused.

In a criminal case, the firing pin impressions of a firearm, broken into number of pieces, was obtained on a lead piece even by hand pressing.

Even the breech marks can be obtained by light hammering on the breech face for comparison as shown in Figures 10.4a and 10.4b.

10.3.2 Use of illegally procured and illegally made firearms

To evade detection from firearm tracing bodies such as the IBIS (Integrated Ballistic Identification System), criminals resort to frequent use of illegally made and illegally procured firearms. This has increased manyfold in recent times. These firearms include improvised, cheap substandard firearms manufactured in clandestine factories and home-made 3D-printed firearms. They often defy known classification and identification criteria and give rise to ambiguous marks that are misleading to unwary experts. In such a case, one has to be either remain non-committal or modify the known identification procedures.

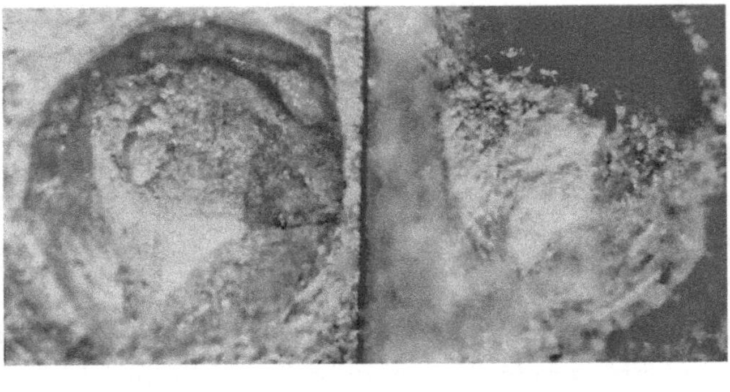

Figure 10.3 Firing pin impression obtained on a lead piece by hand pressing

Figure 10.4a Breech marks obtained by light hammering on breech face

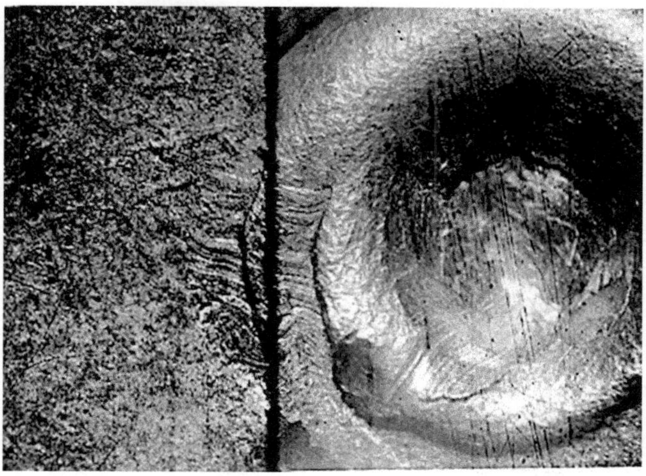

Figure 10.4b Matching of breech marks on evidence empty and test specimen

10.3.3 Deceptive similar or dissimilar marks on fired or unfired ammunition – needs caution

Besides the intentional acts of criminals to evade detection, one comes across many instances where misleading similar and dissimilar marks are present on the fired cartridges and bullets that need objective evaluation. The expert needs to be cautious while forming opinions in such cases. Some such illustrative examples are cited below.

- Deceptive identifiable breech marks on the primer of the seized empty. This was created during the push–fit operation of primers during the manufacture of a particular lot of ammunition (Figure 10.5). It was not due to the breech of

Figure 10.5 Deceptive breech marks created during push–fit operation of primers at the time of manufacturing

the firearm. This needs an objective assessment to evaluate such misleading marks before forming a correct and guarded option.

With the advent of digital imaging systems, obtaining direct impressions of the firing pin and breech face is significantly simplified.

- Deceptive class characteristic rifling marks on the fired bullet due to rifling of an undersized .29″ barrel of a .32″ revolver. This leads to misleading class characteristic marks on the fired bullet that do not match with the class characteristic marks of the barrel. This needs objective evaluation before forming an opinion.
- Deceptive double firing pin hits due to excessive play of spring-driven firing pin of a 12-bore SBBL shotgun. This may lead to a wrong opinion that one of the hits was a misfired hit (Figure 10.6).

From the above deliberations, it is evident that the present era of forensic firearm identification is an era of frequent unforeseen challenges of misleading and ambiguous exhibits in firearm cases. This requires up-to-date knowledge of the changing modus operandi of criminals and also of those firearms that are likely to create unusual,

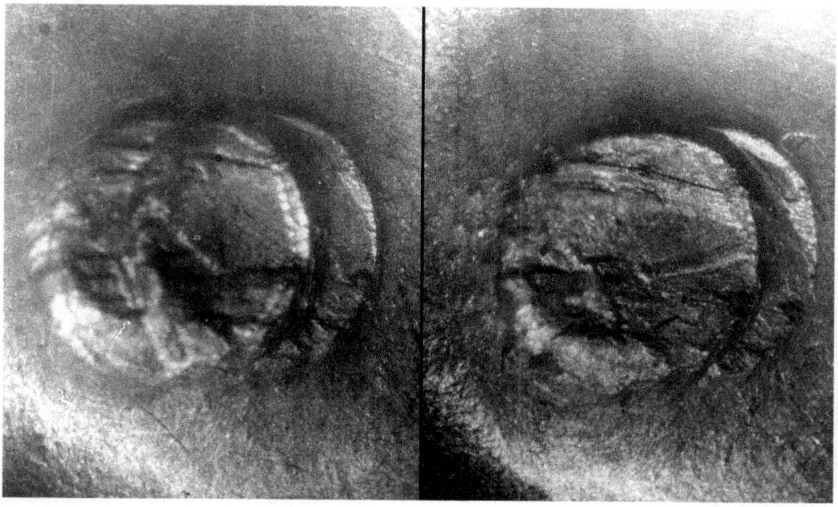

Figure 10.6 Double firing pin hits

misleading and ambiguous marks on their fired ammunition. These include substandard firearms that are manufactured in clandestine factories. One is liable to form a wrong opinion if an attempt is made to form a positive or negative (definite) opinion despite insufficient identifying marks. The expert must not be too keen to form a definite positive/negative opinion. Obviously, such an overenthusiastic expert would contribute to creating unfounded doubts about the testability and reliability of the science of firearm identification. A scientific expert is a neutral witness assisting the court to establish the truth with its scientific opinion. Therefore, the most important rider for a zero-error opinion is the expertise of the examiner who is entrusted to form an opinion. It is thus apparent that for a possible zero-error opinion, besides choice of appropriate test cartridges, similar and dissimilar marks on the evidence empty need objective evaluation of the source that created the marks to come to a right conclusion. This will prove helpful in minimizing error while forming opinions.

11

Identification of rifled firearms from fired bullets

Bullets found inside the victim's body or at the crime scene provide valuable evidentiary clues to connect the crime with the criminal through the weapon of offence. Once the suspected firearm is seized, it can be ascertained whether it is the one that fired the bullets/bullet pieces that were recovered. This calls for the search and seizure of the suspected firearm. The expert is therefore confronted foremost with the task of ascertaining the calibre, make and model of the rifled firearm from the fired bullet/bullet pieces seized during investigation.

11.1 Usual and unusual class characteristic marks

It is well known that bullets fired from rifled firearms (pistols, revolvers, rifles, etc.) are engraved with the class characteristic rifling marks: direction of rifling, width of lands and grooves, depth of grooves, angle and pitch of rifling, etc. The class characteristic rifling data of various makes and models of rifled firearms is well documented and kept updated by laboratory personnel. The data enables the expert to ascertain the probable make and model of the suspected firearm from the fired evidence bullet. This helps the investigator to search for the probable firearm, eliminating others.

11.1.1 Unusual class characteristic marks

It poses a problem if the ammunition is mismatched, or the firearm involved is mismatched. Rifled firearms or non-standard firearms that are illegally made in clandestine factories or homemade do not conform to standard specifications. This is even more so if it is a smooth-bore

DOI: 10.4324/9781351023863-14

illegally made firearm especially designed to load and fire rifled ammunition. Bullets fired from these firearms do not carry ordered rifling marks, and it therefore becomes difficult to determine the probable type of firearm and in some cases even the calibre of the firearm from fired bullets. The calibre of the bullet may not necessarily signify the calibre of the involved mismatched firearm. Details of identifying class and individual characteristic marks on bullets fired from such non-standard firearms are out of the purview of the current text. A brief description of new class characteristic parameters for identifying unusual non-standard rifled/smooth-bore firearms from fired bullets has been incorporated for forming opinion to eliminate the improbable and lay hands on the probable suspected firearms.

11.1.1.1 Mismatched ammunition fired from rifled-bore firearms

There are regular factory-made rifled firearms conforming to standard specifications that can load and fire mismatched cartridges of a different bore. Their relative bullet–bore diameter markedly influences class and individual characteristics marks. For an effective search and seizure of the suspected firearm, it is essential to designate the suspected firearm as under-size or over-size in relation to the nominal bullet bore. A .30–06 rifle capable of loading and firing mismatched Winchester .270 cartridges may be referred as a non-standard .270 over-sized .30–06 rifle for the purpose of barrel marks and trajectory evaluation. In addition to being under-/over-sized, the bullet diameter of mismatched ammunition on setup or otherwise may correspond to appropriate ammunition. They may be designated by both the bullet and the firearm such as a .303 bullet fired from a .32–40 rifle.

11.1.1.2 Mismatched non-standard rifled firearms

Cheap, illegally made rifled firearms are often designed to fire pistol, revolver or rifle cartridges of a specific calibre. Their barrels are rifled, but their bore diameter may not necessarily correspond to the designated calibre of the firearm. They may even be under-sized or over-sized throughout their travel inside the rifled barrel. Therefore, the class characteristic rifling marks on bullets fired from such mismatched rifled firearms are unlike those fired from rifled firearms using appropriate ammunition. The nature of rifling/striation marks may identify the type of mismatched firearm.

Deep irregular and partial rifling engravings

Lead bullets fired from an excessively under-sized rifled-bore firearm are likely to be elongated while passing through an abnormally small diameter barrel. The process of elongation and the high velocity of the forward motion of the bullet tend to deflect it from the path and direction of the rifling; consequently, such bullets may not engage the rifling properly. Moreover, the bullet is also shaved during the process of elongation, and shaving is likely to imprint mixed land and groove marks without any clear demarcation.

Almost proper rifling

Sometimes the bullet may engage the mismatched rifling properly. Available class characteristic marks may identify the probable calibre, make and model of the involved mismatched firearm.

Random, discontinuous/insignificant striations

It may not be possible to ascertain whether an over-sized rifled firearm or a non-standard, over-sized smooth-bore firearm is involved.

Figure 11.1 Rifling marks on a .32 elongated lead bullet fired from an under-sized (.29″) revolver

11.1.1.3 Non-standard smooth-bore firearms designed to fire pistols, revolver and rifle cartridges

There is no pre-assigned spiral path in smooth-bore firearms that are designed to load and fire rifle cartridges. Bullets fired from such smooth-bore firearms do not carry orderly barrel marks like those of rifled-bore barrels. They are continuous/discontinuous striae, parallel straight/inclined striae, insignificant striae, groove-like engravings, etc. The nature of the striae pattern on fired bullets identifies the following class characteristic parameters of non-standard smooth-bore firearms:

- Continuous straight/inclined striations indicate under-sized smooth-bore barrel.
- Initial inclined barrel contact indicates misaligned over-sized smooth-bore firearm.
- Reduced diameter of the fired bullet indicates undersize bore diameter of smooth-bore firearm.

11.1.1.4 3D-printed guns

With the advent of easy availability and affordable 3D printers, the making of functional 3D-printed guns at home has become a reality using 3D modelling by CAD (computer-aided design).

The first metal 3D-printed gun has reportedly been printed by Solid Concepts, Texas, USA. It replicated the popular Browning M1911 pistol. The replicated printed Browning metal pistol was strong enough to fire about 50 rounds accurately from the mounted position.

To make the cost low and to evade complicated printing processes, the tensile strength of the construction materials, especially of the barrel and action, of 3D printed guns may not be comparable to their

Figure 11.2 Straight striations on under-sized smooth-bore fired bullets

counterpart guns. There also may be wide variation in the dimensions of their parts such as barrel length, bore diameter, chamber shape, rifling, etc. Depending on the availability of the ammunition, the constructional features (dimensions) of the printed guns may be custom-made by making necessary changes in the available software. These features may vary from one printed gun to another by the same 3D printer. The barrel may be rifled as well as unrifled (smooth bore) for firing rifled ammunition; the barrel length may be short irrespective of the ammunition, to aid concealment, and so on.

Despite being capable of enforcing a tight manufacturing tolerance, 3D-printed guns may not necessarily conform to the specified dimensions and constructional materials of counterpart conventional firearms that are legally manufactured. Most 3D-printed guns that are likely to be encountered in crime would fall into the category of unusual firearms, similar to a product of a clandestine gun factory. Depending on the changes in the available software, the quality of 3D-printed guns may vary; some may even correspond closely to their counterpart rifled- or smooth-bore firearms. The class characteristic marks would vary accordingly as detailed above.

11.2 Individual characteristic rifling marks

Ways of identifying rifled firearms from individual characteristic rifling marks are well known and have been detailed in the preceding sections in varied contexts that include the methodologies adopted for examining and forming opinions. It is necessary to identify the issues to minimize the error.

11.3 Interfering marks on fired bullets

Bullets recovered from the victim's body often get mutilated, deformed or broken. They may not carry all lands and grooves even when they are deformed. They may carry extraneous marks due to striking at bones and other body parts during their passage through the body. These extraneous marks will remain present during the examination and comparison of the evidence bullet.

There are other sources of interfering marks on the evidence bullets:

i. One may find interfering tool marks created on the evidence bullet if extracted by forceps that are not rubber tipped. Use of rubber-tipped or similar forceps will minimize interfering marks on the evidence bullet. This in turn will minimize error during examination of the evidence bullet in this respect.
ii. If the bullet, after passing through the body or without hitting the victim, strikes another object such as a wall, household items, tree, etc. and becomes lodged, then additional marks of the extracting tool may interfere with the rifling marks if due care is not taken. The bullet should be removed after making enough space surrounding the lodged bullet for easy extraction.

12

Scientific evidence vs eyewitness in criminal trials involving firearms

Eyewitness and scientific evidence play a vital role in the judicious decision of the criminal trial. The importance of scientific evidence in criminal incidents of gunfire is well recognized worldwide. Eyewitness evidence is even discarded if it is inconsistent with the medical and ballistic expert report, if relevant and reliable. It is worthwhile to discuss their relative merits in the present scenario of criminal justice system.

12.1 Eyewitness evidence

The eyewitness who narrates the shooting incident during the criminal trial is the prime witness of the criminal incident. Being direct evidence of witnessing the criminal incident, the testimony of an eyewitness is usually considered to be superior evidence compared to any other evidence placed before the court. Conviction or acquittal of the accused more often depends on the testimony of the eyewitness and whether the eyewitness is reliable and trustworthy.

12.1.1 Merits of oral testimony of eyewitness

Oral testimony may broadly be classified into three categories, namely:

- wholly reliable
- wholly unreliable
- neither wholly reliable nor wholly unreliable.

DOI: 10.4324/9781351023863-15

While discussing their relative merits, the Supreme Court of India in case *Thevar v. State of Madras* (1957) has held:

> In the first category of proof, the court should have no difficulty in coming to its conclusion either way – it may convict or may acquit on the testimony of a single witness, if it is found to be above reproach or suspicion of interestedness, incompetence or subornation. In the second category, the court equally has no difficulty in coming to its conclusion. It is in the third category of cases, that the court has to be circumspect and has to look for corroboration in material particulars by reliable testimony, direct or circumstantial.

12.1.2 Trustworthiness of eyewitness

In addition to the reliability of the oral testimony, the trustworthiness of the eyewitness, whether interested, biased or trustworthy, is an equally important factor in the decision of the case. It is worthwhile to cite some of the court judgments on the probative values of the eyewitnesses.

An eyewitness of the shooting incident may be:

i. The victim (injured or unhurt)

While discussing the probative value of the victim as eyewitness, the Supreme Court of India in the case *Abdul Syeed v. State of Madhya Pradesh* (2010) held:

> The question of the weight to be attached to the evidence of a witness that was himself injured in the course of the occurrence has been extensively discussed by this Court. Where a witness to the occurrence has himself been injured in the incident, the testimony of such a witness is generally considered to be very reliable, as he is a witness that comes with a built-in guarantee of his presence at the scene of the crime and is unlikely to spare his actual assailant(s) in order to falsely implicate someone. "Convincing evidence is required to discredit an injured witness."

ii. Victim's relations and friends

> It is a settled law that natural witnesses cannot be labelled as interested witnesses. Interested witnesses are those who want to derive some

> benefit out of the litigation/case. If the circumstances reveal that a witness had witnessed the crime, his deposition cannot be discarded merely on the ground of being closely related to the victim/deceased.

The Supreme Court in the case *Braham Swaroop and another v. State of U.P.* (2010) held:

> Merely because the witnesses were close relatives of the deceased, their testimonies cannot be discarded. Their relationship to one of the parties is not a factor that effects the credibility of a witness, more so, a relation would not conceal the actual culprit and make allegations against an innocent person. A party has to lay down a factual foundation and prove by leading impeccable evidence in respect of its false implication. However, in such cases, the Court has to adopt a careful approach and analyse the evidence to find out whether it is cogent and credible evidence.

iii. Onlookers/strangers (firing at public places)

The Supreme Court of India in the case *Dandu Jaggaraju v. State of A.P.* (2011) held:

> We also see that the last seen evidence of P.Ws. 2, 3 and 6 is equally uncertain. Significantly, the statements of P.Ws.2 and 3 were recorded by the Magistrate for the first time under Section 164 about four months after the alleged incident and though both witnesses had deposed that they would be able to identify the appellant who was otherwise a stranger to them, no effort had been made to hold a test identification parade. Mr. Mahesh Babu has, however, placed reliance on the statement of P.W. 6 who is stated to be a completely independent witness. Even this witness had testified that he did not know the appellant personally but he still claimed that he had seen the appellant at the bus depot on the day in question along with the deceased and that he was called upon to identify him for the first time in Court when his statement was recorded on the 4th of November, 2004 which was two and a half years after the murder.

It was held that the testimonies of these witnesses did not inspire confidence and hence acquittal.

iv. Assailant's friends and relations (firing at assailant's place)
v. Chance witness to the incident: friends and relations

12.2 Scientific evidence

Scientific evidence relates to the specialized field of forensic ballistics and forensic medicine. Scientific evidence has the added advantage that the court can see and examine factual items of physical exhibits that are related to the commission of the crime. The court can also examine and interpret the testimony of the forensic expert on the findings of scientific analysis of the physical exhibits for the purpose of assessing scientific proof on issues related to the crime. The reliability of firearm evidence has already been discussed at length in the preceding paragraphs.

12.2.1 Trustworthiness of expert's evidence

The only issue that needs to be established is whether the expert is trustworthy. In the present legal system, a scientific expert is considered to be trustworthy and creditable because:

i. Forensic scientists are truly neutral court witnesses whether appearing for the prosecution or the defence, and hence trusted witnesses to assist the court in their field of expertise.
ii. Forensic scientists are especially skilled, well trained, experienced and highly qualified professionals, and hence can be treated as experts in the field.
iii. The presumed impartiality and objectivity of forensic experts to reveal the truth by the application of scientific methods makes the scientific evidence trustworthy and worth consideration.

A combined reading of the above reveals that it is worth becoming acquainted with the determinative points or issues that leads the court to convict or acquit the accused on the merits and demerits of eyewitness and scientific evidence. Some of the relevant case judgment excerpts are as follows.

12.2.2 Sole evidence of eyewitness believed to award conviction

The Supreme Court of India in the case *Ajay v. State of Bihar* (2000) held:

> We, in fact, see no reason as to why, though, the weapon was snatched from Ajay, as stated by P.W. 2, yet the investigating agency never

sent the same to the Ballistic Expert for being examined, and produced the report before the Court. But on that sole ground, it may not be possible for us to discard the trustworthy testimony of two eye-witnesses, who have unequivocally indicated that the two accused Ajay and Dacha came on a motor cycle and fired from the respective weapon, which hit the deceased. Contentions having been advanced on the reliability of P.Ws. 1 and 2, though ordinarily, we do not reappreciate the evidence, when two Courts of fact have appreciated and relied upon the same, yet we have gone through the evidence of two eye-witnesses P.Ws. 1 and 2. We do not find anything brought out in their cross-examination to impeach their testimony in any manner so as to affect the substratum of the prosecution case in relation to the two accused Ajay and Bacha coming on a motor cycle, and fired at the deceased from the respective weapon. We, therefore, hold the two aforesaid witnesses to be wholly trustworthy and the Courts below rightly relied upon their testimony to bring home the charge against the two accused appellants.

12.2.3 Testimony of eyewitness corroborated by medical and ballistic evidence believed for convicting the accused

The Supreme court in the case *Nachhattar Singh v. State of Punjab* (1975) held:

> The conviction of the appellant mainly rests on the evidence of Bhagwan Kaur, PW 2 which had been corroborated in material particulars by independent evidence, including that of the Ballistic Expert, Mr. J.K. Sinha [...]
>
> The High Court found Bhagwan Kaur credit-worthy and we have no good reason to differ from that conclusion.
>
> Bhagwan Kaur's version with regard to the nature of the inflicting weapon and the manner of causing the fatal injuries to Dan Singh stood corroborated by the medical testimony. Dr. Jagjit Singh, PW 1, who conducted the autopsy noted six gunshot wounds on the body of the deceased. He found wadding and card-board pieces embedded in Injuries 1 and 2, and blackening on the margins of Injury 3, indicating that those injuries were caused from close range.
>
> Then, there was the testimony of Mr. J K Sinha, Ballistic Expert, who after examination of the empties (which were found at the scene of

murder on December 18) and the licensed gun of the appellant, opined that those empties had been fired through the barrel of this gun.

Mr. Singh, however, contends that no empty cartridges had, in fact, been found at the spot, and that this circumstantial evidence had been fabricated after the arrest of the appellant and seizure of the gun which took place on December 19. [...] The Courts below have for cogent reasons rejected the defense contention and accepted the prosecution version that the appellant was taken into custody along with his gun, on December 24. We find no fault with that reasoning. The gun having been seized by the police on the 24th, there was no scope for fabrication, nor any ground for doubting the genuineness of the empties picked up from the scene on December 18, and which on December 24, were no longer in the possession or control of the investigating officer. They were, as deposed to by Shri J.K Sinha, PW 12, in the possession of the Forensic Laboratory since December [...] Thus the ballistic evidence confirmed the connection of the appellant with the crime.

Suffice it to say, that excepting the evidence with regard to the motive, the appellant has not been able to assail the appreciation of the evidence done by the High Court on any solid ground. We, therefore, confirm the finding that the appellant was the person who had shot dead Dan Singh in the manner alleged by the prosecution. The appeal fails and is dismissed.

12.2.4 Eyewitness testimony of brother of the deceased as an interested witness not believed: no independent corroborative firearm evidence was submitted – acquittal

The Supreme Court of India in the case *State of Punjab v. Sukhwant Singh* (1995) held:

> There is yet another infirmity in this case. We find that whereas an empty had been recovered by PW6, ASI Raghubir Singh from the spot and a pistol along with some cartridges were seized from the possession of the appellant at the time of his arrest, yet the prosecution, for reasons best known to it, did not send the recovered empty and the seized pistol to the ballistic expert for the examination and expert opinion. Comparison could have provided link evidence between the crime and the accused. This again is an omission on the part of the prosecution for which no explanation has been furnished either in the trial court or

before us. It hardly needs to be emphasized that in cases where injuries are caused by fire arms, the opinion of the Ballistic Expert is of a considerable importance where both the fire arm and the crime cartridge are recovered during the investigation to connect an accused with the crime. Failure to produce the expert opinion before the trial court in such cases affects the creditworthiness of the prosecution case to a great extent.

From a critical analysis of the material on the record, we find that it would not be safe to rely upon the sole testimony of PW3 Gurmej Singh, the brother of the deceased, without independent corroboration in view of the infirmities pointed out by us above which render his testimony as not wholly reliable and since in the present case no such independent corroboration is available on the record, it would be unsafe to rely upon the testimony of PW3 only to uphold the conviction of the appellant. The prosecution has not been able to establish the case against the appellant beyond a reasonable doubt. The trial court, therefore, fell in error in convicting and sentencing the appellant. His conviction and sentence cannot be sustained. […] The conviction and sentence of the appellant is set aside.

12.2.5 Eyewitness inconsistent with medical and ballistic evidence – acquittal

The Supreme Court of India in the case *Ram Narain v. State of Punjab* (1975) held:

Thus a combined reading of the evidence of Dr. Walia, the medical expert, and Mr. J K Sinha, ballistics expert, clearly establishes that the deceased died of two gunshot injuries and the prosecution has not been able to explain this important circumstance. For these reasons, therefore, the evidence of two eyewitnesses, Surjit Singh and Joginder Singh, is wholly inconsistent with the medical evidence, so also the evidence of ballistic expert and must be rejected on that ground alone, apart from other inherent improbabilities which appear in their evidence and which have already been pointed out.

Where thus the evidence of the witness is wholly inconsistent with the medical evidence or the evidence of the ballistic expert, this is a most fundamental defect in the prosecution case and unless reasonably explained it is sufficient to discredit it the entire case.

A combined reading of the aforesaid excerpts of judgments clearly reveals that the significant determinative points or issues which led the court to convict or acquit the accused are generally:

i. Whether the eyewitness is trustworthy.
ii. Whether scientific evidence to corroborate, prove or disprove issues/determinative points are relevant and reliable and court's view on eyewitness vs scientific evidence.
iii. Whether medical and ballistics expert evidence is inconsistent with the eyewitness evidence.

While discussing the relative significance of eyewitness and scientific evidence, the Supreme Court of India held in the case *Gurucharan Singh v. State of Punjab* (1962):

> There is no inflexible rule to the effect that the prosecution could succeed in proving the charge of murder alleged to have been caused with a lethal weapon only if an expert is examined. Where the direct evidence is of an unimpeachable character and the nature of the injuries disclosed by the post-mortem reports is clearly consistent with the direct evidence, the examination of a ballistics expert may not be essential. Contrarily, the evidence of a ballistics expert would assume significance where direct evidence is not satisfactory, or is of interested witnesses or where the nature of the injuries requires expert corroboration. In other words, whether the examination of a ballistics expert is necessary is dependent upon the factual context as it emerges in each case.

Selected references

Ajay v. State of Bihar (2000) AIR 2000SC 3538 (India)

Bhupendrasinh A v. Chudasama v State of Gujrat, 4.11.97, AIR 1997 SC 3790, SCI (India)

Brahmswaroop and another v. State of UP, reported in AIR 2011 SC 28 (India)

Com v. Pytou Heang, 458 Mass. 827, 837–38, 942 N.E.2d 927, 938 (2011) (USA)

Com v. Pytou Heang, 458 Mass. 827, 846–50, 942 N.E.2d 927, 944–47 (2011) (USA)

Dack, J. R. (2014). *Using Forensic Ballistics in the Courtroom*. Student Works. 637. https://scholarship.shu.edu/student_scholarship/637.

Dandu Jaggaraju v. State of A.P. (2011) SC2011 (AIR 2011SC 3387) (India)

Darshan Singh v. State of Punjab (2010) 2 SCC 333 (India)

Daubert v. Merrell Dow Pharmaceuticals, Inc. (1993) 509 U.S. 579 (USA)

Evans v. Commonwealth, 230 KY. 411, 19 S.W. 2d 1091 (1929) (USA)

Ex. CT. Mahadev vs DG Border Security force 2002 SCC Sc 739/14-06-2002

Frye v. United States (1923) 293 F. 1013 (D.C. Cir. 1923) (USA)

Ghudan v. State of Madhya Pradesh (2003) 12 SCC 485 (India)

Godard, C. (1930) The Valentine's Day Massacre: A study in Ammunition tracing. *American Journal of Police Science*, *12*(1), 60–78.

Gorman, M. A. (1987). Evaluating eyewitness testimony in criminal trials. *Chicago-Kent Law Review*, *63*(1), article 7.

Gurucharan Singh v. State of Punjab (1962), Supreme Court of India, cited by Supreme Court in *Rajesh v. State of Haryana*, 1648 of 2019, vide para 29 pp. 35–36. https://main.sci.gov.in/supremecourt/2019/14406/14406_2019_34_1501_24606_Judgement_03-Nov-2020.pdf

Hamby, J. E., Brundage, D. J., & Thorpe, J. W. (2009). The Identification of Bullets Fired from 10 Consecutively Rifled 9mm Ruger Pistol Barrels: A Research Project Involving 507 Participants from 20 Countries. *AFTE Journal*, *41*(2), 99–110.

Hays, S. R. (1959) Ballistics: A study of the expert witness. *William & Mary Law Review*, *2*(1), article 5.

Hema v. State of Tamilnadu (2013) (10) SCC192 (India)

Jauhari, M. & Sinha, J. K. (1962) Wounding effect of a spherical shot falling under gravity. *Journal of Forensic Sciences USA*, 7(3), 345–350.

Joginder Singh v. State of Haryana (2013) AIR SCW 6169 (India)

Nachhattar Singh v. State of Punjab, 1975 CLJ 66 SC (India)

People v. Lasko, 23 Cal. 4th. 101, 96 Cal. Rptr. 2d 441, 999P.2d 666 (2000) (USA)

Raj Kumar v. State of Haryana (13-06-1996- PNHC)MANU/PH/0916/1996

Ram Narain Singh v. Punjab (1975) 1975 AIR 1727, 1976SCR (1) 27 (India)

Robert R. Brown v. USA (1921) 256 U.S. 335 (USA)

Ronnie Clark v. State of Louisiana (2003) Court of Appeal, 5th Circuit (USA)

State v. Campbell, 213 Iowa 677, 693, 239 N.W. 715, 723 (1931) (USA)

State (Delhi) v. Jasbir Chauhan, Sessions Court (February 2015) (India)

State of Himachal Pradesh v. Jai Lal (1999) AIR 1999 SC3318 (India)

State of Karnataka v. Yarappa Reddy (1999) 8 SCC 715 (India)

State through CBI, New Delhi v. S J Chaudhary (1996) Criminal Law Journal, 1713, SC (India)

Sukhwant Singh v. Punjab (1995) AIR, 1995 SCC suppl. (2) 262 (India)

Suresh Singhal v. State (Delhi Administration) Criminal Appeal no. 1548 of 2011 (India)

United States v. Glynn, 578 F.Supp.2d 567, 574–575 (S.D.N.Y. 2008) (USA)

United States v. Green, 405 F.Supp.2d 104, 124 (D. Mass. 2005) (USA)

United States v. Natson, 469 F.Supp.2d 1253, 1261–1262 (M.D. Ga. 2007) (USA)

United States v. Monteiro, 407 F. Supp.2d 351, 374 (D. Mass. 2006) (USA)

United States Department of Justice (2023, December). Uniform language for testimony and reports for the forensic firearms/tool-marks discipline pattern examination. www.justice.gov/olp/forensic-science#ultr

United States Department of Justice (2013). United States Department of Justice Statement on the PCAST Report: Forensic Science in Criminal Courts: Ensuring Scientific Validity of Feature-Comparison Methods. www.justice.gov/media/1116366/dl?inline

Index

Note: *Italic* page numbers refer to figures and page numbers followed by "n" denote endnotes

Abdul Syeed v. State of Madhya Pradesh 115–16
accidental firing 89–91
acquittals: guiding principles 55; negative opinion and 52
action mechanism 46–8, 70–1
admissibility of expert opinion and testimony: changes and issues in 6–8; *see also* India; USA
admitted firing: accidental 89–91; into air to celebrate occasion 94–5; self-defence 91–4
Ajay v. State of Bihar 117–18
assault rifles 51, 78, *79*
auto loaders *see* self-loading firearms (semi-/fully automatic)

BalScan system 32
barrel: functional parts of 45–6 uniqueness of 6; *see also* microscopic examination
big game shots 58–9
blown or perforated caps 66–7
body: of firearm (*see* action mechanism); of victim (*see* victim's body/wound)
bolt-action rifles 75–6, 79, 90
Braham Swaroop and another v. State of U.P. 116
breech marks 100, 103, 104, 105–6
Brown vs. United States 91
buckshot 58–9, 60
bullets: as evidentiary clues 56–8; and pellets (shots), compared 56; *see also* rifled firearms identification from fired bullets

calibre/bore of firearm 45, 46; ascertaining 50
cartridge cases, rifled and smooth-bore 50

cartridges: general makeup of 48–9; low- or high-velocity firearms 51; manually or auto loaded firearms 51; shotgun 72–3
CERN: determination of statistical certainty 17–18
choke - shotgun muzzle dimension 73
class characteristic rifling marks 56–7, 58; usual and unusual 108–12
close range fire 60, 65, 67–8, 82
cocking and firing 47, 70–1
Code of Criminal Procedure, Section 293 (1973), India 36–9
competent experts, identifying 29–33
crime scene 84
criminal intent, establishing 87–8
criminal modus operandi to avoid detection 101–4
cross-examination: India 39; US 7, 31

Dandu Jaggaraju v. State of A.P. 116
Darshan Singh v. State of Punjab 92
date and time of incident, eyewitness statements and investigative leads 84–5
Daubert standard 7, 9–13, 23
deceptive perception of empty magazine and accidental firing 90
deceptive simultaneous similar or dissimilar marks 103, 105–7
delay in forwarding evidence 53
Department of Justice, US: guidelines for government examiners 13–14; PCAST report 34
digital imaging systems 106
dispersion of spherical shots/pellets 59–62, 73
distance of fire: eyewitness statement 81, 82; and position of firer, wads 63–4, 65; postmortem examination 82; powder tattooing 47–8, 67–8; *see also* dispersion of spherical shots/pellets
double-action revolvers 74–5, 90–1
double-barrelled shotgun (DBBL) 72, 79

empty magazine: deceptive perception and accidental firing 90
empty shells and fired bullets 20–1, 22, 28, 39; *see also* fired empty
Evans v. Commonwealth 5–6, 21–2, 88
Evidence Act: Section 45, India 35–6, 39
evidence in criminal trials (overview) 3–9
evidentiary values: and classification of firearms 70–9; *see also* fired empty (evidentiary values)
expert opinion: distance of fire 61; post-mortem examination 82; type of firearm/recovery 57, 58
expert opinion and testimony 4–5, 6; changes and issues in admissibility of 6–8
extraction and ejection of fired empty 48, 70, 71
extraneous marks 32, 112
eyewitness evidence/statements 43, 114; misuse/misleading 4; oral testimony of 3, 114–15; trustworthiness of expert evidence and 117–21; trustworthiness of 115–16
eyewitness evidence/statements and investigative leads 81; on date and

time of incident 84–5; on firing at victim/physical clues 81–2; on functioning of firearm during incident 83; identitification of perpetrator 85–7; on motive or reason for firing at victim 87–8; place of occurrence 83–4

Federal Rule of Evidence 702 10, 11–13, 29
firearm and ammunition, basic understanding of 47–9
firearm identification from fired empties: clarity of marks on test cartridges 100–1; interfering marks on test cartridges 99–100; misleading examination and comparison of marks 101–7; *see also* fired empty (evidentiary values); rifled firearms identification from fired bullets
firearm type: classification 71–9; eyewitness statement 81, 83; postmortem examination 82
firearm–ammunition linkage 12–13, 51, 53–4, 66; and uniqueness of barrel 5–6
fired empty, extraction and ejection of 48, 70, 71
fired empty (evidentiary values) 50–2; continuity of chain of evidence - recovery of fired empty, genuine or doubtful 52–4; firearm type 79–80; identification of type of firearm 50–2; lapses and acquittal - guiding principles 55; recovered firearm and empty not sent for expert opinion 54, *see also* firearm identification from fired empties
fired projectiles as evidentiary clues 56; bullets 56–8; primer 66–7; propellants 67–9; spherical shots/ pellets and dispersion 58–62, 73; wads 62–5
firing pin 47, 66–7; deceptive double 106; marks *99*, 100; replacing 101–3; tampering with 103, 104
first information report (FIR) 43, 84–5
Frye standard 10, 11

general perception 28–9
Ghudan v. State of Madhya Pradesh 53
Godard, C. 5–6, 21–2
Gorman, M. A. 87
grooved bore firearms *see* rifled firearms
grooves and lands 16, 45, 56–7, 108, 112
grudge against victim and misuse of right to self-defence 93–4
gunshot residue (GSR) 66

Hamby, J. E. et al. 21, 34
hand grip/hand guns 48
Hema v. State of Tamilnadu 55
high-velocity firearms *see* low- or high-velocity firearms
hunting rifles 51
hunting shots, big and small game 58–9

illegally manufactured/procured firearms 30–1, 32, 104, 107, 108–9, 112
India: admissibility of expert evidenceSection 45 of Evidence Act and expert evidence 35–6, 39; Section 293 of Code of Criminal Procedure (1973) 36–9

India, changes in rules of evidence and admissibility of expert evidence 6–7
Indian Penal Code (IPC): Sections 96 & 97 91–2
indirect evidence 4
interested witness 119–20
interfering marks on test cartridges 99–100
investigative aspects 43–9
investigative lapses and court rulings 53–5

Joginder Singh v. State of Haryana 52

Kalashnikov assault rifles 78, *79*

LG shots 58–9
licensed firearms 46, 51, 58, 71
loading and locking 46–7, 70–1
low- or high-velocity firearms 51; shape and size of propellant for differentiation of 68–9

manually operated firearms 51, 71–5
marriage ceremonies, firing into air to celebrate 94–5
medical and ballistic evidence: corroborated by eyewitness testimony 118–19; inconsistent with eyewitness testimony 120
medical help 81–2
medico-legal reports 48, 82; Evidence Act: Section 45, India 36; wads recovered from body 65
microscopic examination: comparison microscope 5, 18–19, 20–1; "smooth-bore barrel" 15–16; training and experience 31–2
misleading examination and comparison of marks 101–7
misleading/ambiguous marks 30–1, 32, 104, 107
mismatched ammunition/ mismatched firearm 108–9
mistaken identity of perpetrator 86–7
misuse of right to self-defence 93–4
misuse/misleading eyewitness statements 4
motive or reason for firing at victim 87–8

Nachhttar Singh v. State of Punjab 87–8, 118–19
National Academy of Sciences/ National Institute of Standard and Technology (NAST/NIST), US 13
negative opinion and acquittal 52
Nihal Singh and Hardial Singh v. State of Punjab 53–4

onlookers/strangers, as eyewitnesses 116
oral testimony of eyewitness 3, 114–15

PCAST report, US Department of Justice 34
pellets *see* spherical shots/pellets
perforated or blown caps 66–7
physical evidence: crime scene 84; investigative aspects of 44–5, 49; lapses and court rulings 53–5; sealed 53, 64, 82; victim's body/ clothing 82
pistols 48, 51; self-loading 77–8
place of occurrence 83–4
post-mortem reports *see* medico-legal reports
potential rate of error: and element of subjectivity 23–5; proficiency testing and 33–4
powder tattooing 47–8, 67–8
pressure, development of 100, 103

primer: as evidentiary clues 66–7; and firing pin marks 99, 100, 101
private and government experts, India 39
proficiency test of identifying marks of consecutively rifled barrels (subclass marks) 34
proficiency test and potential rate of error 33–4
propellants, as evidentiary clues 67–9
propelling of projectile and gaseous discharge residues 47–8
protection of fellow officer and reliable eyewitness, self-defence 92–3
pump-action shotguns 76, 77

Raj Kumar v. State of Haryana 88
Ram Narain Singh v. State of Punjab 86, 120
recovery of firearm 85–6; and seized evidence bullet 58
reliability and testability issues 6, 21–3
reliable eyewitness, protection of fellow officer and 92–3
reliable opinion, interpreting scientific analysis for achieving 25–7
repeater firearms 75–6, 79, 80, 90
research orientation 31
revolvers 48, 51, 74–5, 79; classification as repeater 75; single- and double-action 74–5, 90–1; trigger pull of 74–5
rifled firearms identification from fired bullets 108; individual characteristic rifling marks 112; interfering marks on fired bullets 112–13; usual and unusual class characteristic marks 108–12
rifled and smooth-bore firearms: cartridge cases 50; compared 45–6; fired projectiles 56
rifles 48
rifling *see* class characteristic rifling marks; rifled firearms identification from fired bullets
rotating cylinder and accidental firing 90–1

St Valentine's Day Massacre 5
scientific evidence 117; admissibility 4–5; changes in laws of evidence and admissibility of expert evidence 6–7; trustworthiness of expert evidence and eyewitness evidence 117–21
sealed physical exhibits 53, 64, 82
search and seizure of fired empty 79–80
self-defence, admitted firing in 91–4
self-loading firearms (semi-/fully automatic) 76–9; cartridge/fired empty 51, 80, 90
service rifles 51
shotguns 46, 48, 51, 71–3, 79; variation in chamber dimension 72–3; variation in muzzle dimension - choke 73; *see also* spherical shots/pellets
shoulder firearms *see* shotguns
similar and dissimilar marks: deceptive simultaneous 103, 105–7; and general perception 27–9
single-barrelled shotgun (SBBL) 72, 79
small game shots 59
smooth-bore firearms 46; designed to fire rifle cartridges 111; "smooth-bore barrel" 15–16; *see also* rifled and smooth-bore firearms; shotguns
spherical shots/pellets: and bullets, compared 56; and dispersion, as evidentiary clues 58–62, 73
State of HP v. Jai Lal 36

State of Karnataka v. K. Yarappa Reddy 55
State of Punjab v. Sukhwant Singh 54, 119–20
State through BCI, New Delhi v. S J Chaudhary 35–6
State v. Jasbir Chauhan 95
statistical significance/certainty: proficiency testing of experts 33–4; of unique identifying features of firearm 17–20
stock and butt/shoulder firearms 48
strangers/onlookers, as eyewitnesses 116
striations: on fired shots/pellets and shotgun cupped cartridge 61–2; matching striations 18–20
striker blow 101
subclass marks 34
subjectivity, potential rate of error and element of 23–5
suspect: apprehension and defence of 43–4; identification of 85–7

test cartridges 99–101
testability and reliability issues 6, 21–3
Thewar v. State of Madras 115
3D-printed guns 111–12
time and date of incident: eyewitness statements and investigative leads 84–5
tolerance limits in manufacturing process, significance of 16–17
training and experience of examining firearms cases 31–3
trigger pull and accidental firing 91
trustworthiness: of expert evidence 117; of eyewitness 115–16

uniqueness of identifying features of firearm 14–23
unserviceable, making firearm 103–4
USA: admissibility of expert evidence 10; changes in rules of evidence and 6–7; Daubert standard 7, 8, 9–13; Department of Justice guidelines for government examiners 13–14; Frye standard 10, 11; identifying competent experts 29–33; interpreting scientific analysis for achieving reliable opinion on firearm–ammunition linkage 25–9; potential rate of error and element of subjectivity 23–5; proficiency test of identifying marks of consecutively rifled barrels (subclass marks) 34; proficiency testing and potential rate of error 33–4; scientific validity of uniqueness of identifying features of firearm 14–23

victim, as eyewitness 115
victim's body/wound: bullets recovered from 112; physical evidence from 82; wads recovered from 64–5, 82
victim's brother as interested witness 119–20
victim's relations or friends, as eyewitnesses 115–16
visibility and identification of perpetrator 85, 86

wads: construction material and number of 62–3; as evidentiary clues 62–5; make-up and location of position of assailant 63–4

For Product Safety Concerns and Information please contact our EU representative GPSR@taylorandfrancis.com
Taylor & Francis Verlag GmbH, Kaufingerstraße 24, 80331 München, Germany

www.ingramcontent.com/pod-product-compliance
Ingram Content Group UK Ltd.
Pitfield, Milton Keynes, MK11 3LW, UK
UKHW020000200926
475702UK00015B/2399